MESSAGES
from the
EPISTLE
to the
HEBREWS

MESSAGES
from the
EPISTLE
to the
HEBREWS

by
H. C. G. Moule

Wipf & Stock
PUBLISHERS
Eugene, Oregon

Wipf and Stock Publishers
199 W 8th Ave, Suite 3
Eugene, OR 97401

Messages from the Epistle to the Hebrews
By Moule, Handley C. G.
ISBN 13: 978-1-55635-456-4
ISBN 10: 1-55635-456-8
Publication date 5/1/2007

CONTENTS

CONTENTS

PREFACE

THE following chapters are the work of intervals of leisure scattered over a long time. The exposition had advanced some way when an unexpected call to new and exacting duties compelled me to put it aside for several years. Accordingly a certain difference of treatment in the later chapters as compared with the earlier will probably be seen by the reader, particularly a rather fuller detail in the exposition. But purpose and plan are essentially the same throughout.

No attempt whatever is made, here or in the course of the work, to deal with those literary and historical problems which so conspicuously attach themselves to this Epistle. Who the "Hebrews" were is nowhere discussed. Nor is any positive answer offered to a question to which assuredly no such answer can be given, the question, namely, of the authorship. In my opinion, in face of all that I have read to the contrary, it still seems at least possible

that the *ultimate* human author was St. Paul.
All, or very nearly all, the objections to his
name which the phenomena of the Epistle
primâ facie present, and some of which lie
unquestionably deep, seem to be capable of
a provisional answer if we assume, what is
so conceivable, that the Apostle committed
his message and its argument, on purpose,
to a colleague so gifted, mentally and by
the Spirit, that he might be trusted to
cast the work into his own style. The well-
known remark of Origen that only God knows
who "wrote" the Epistle appears to me to
point (if we look at its context) this way.
Origen surely means by the "writer" what
is meant in Rom. xvi. 22. Only, on the
hypothesis, the amanuensis of our Epistle was,
for a special purpose presumably, a Christian
prophet in his own right.

In any case the author, if not an apostle,
was a prophet. And he carries to us a prophet's
"burthen" of unspeakable import, and in words
to which all through the Christian ages the soul
has responded as to the words of the Holy Spirit.

STUDIES IN HEBREWS

1

Consider Him

Hebrews 1-2

L ET us open the Epistle to the Hebrews, with
an aim simple and altogether practical for
heart and for life. Let us take it just as it
stands, and somewhat as a whole. We will not
discuss its authorship, interesting and extensive
as that problem is. We will not attempt,
within the compass of a few short chapters,
to expound continuously its wonderful text.
Rather, we will gather up from it some of its
large and conspicuous spiritual messages, taken
as messages of the Word of God "which liveth
and abideth for ever."

No part of Holy Scripture is ever really out

of date. But it is true meanwhile that, as for
persons so for periods, there are Scripture books
and Scripture truths which are more than
ordinarily timely. It is not that others are
therefore untimely, nor that only one class of
book or one aspect of truth can be eminently
timely at one time. But it seems evident that
the foreseeing Architect of the Bible has so
adjusted the parts of His wonderful vehicle of
revelation and blessing that special fitnesses
continually emerge between our varying times
and seasons on the one hand and the multifold
Word on the other.

The Epistle to the Hebrews is in some remarkable respects a book timely for our day. It
invites to itself, if I read it aright, the renewed
attention of the thoughtful Christian, and not
least of the thoughtful Christian of the English
Church, as it brings him messages singularly in
point to some of the main present needs of his
spiritual life and its surroundings. It was
written manifestly in the first instance to meet
special and pressing current trials; it bears the
impress of a time of severe sifting, a time when
foundations were challenged, and individual faith
put to even agonizing proofs, and the community
threatened with an almost dissolution. Such a
writing must have a voice articulate and sympathetic for a period like ours.

We will take into our hands then, portion by
portion, this wonderful "open letter," and listen
through it to some of the things which "the
Spirit saith " to the saints and to the Church.
We now contemplate in this sense the first
two chapters. We put quite aside a host of
points of profound interest in detail, and ask
ourselves only what is the broad surface, the drift
and total, of the message here. As to its climax,
it is JESUS CHRIST, our "merciful and faithful
High Priest " (ii. 17). As to the steps that
lead up to the climax, they are a presentation of
the personal glory of Jesus Christ, as God the Son
of God, as Man the Son of Man, who for us men
and our salvation came, suffered, and prevailed.

Who that reads the Bible with the least care
has not often noted this in the first passages of
the Hebrews, and could not at once so state the
matter ? What is the great truth of Hebrews i. ?
Jesus Christ is GOD (ver. 8) ; the Son (ver. 2) ;
absolutely *like* the Father (ver. 3) ; Lord of the
bright Company of Heaven, who in all their
ranks and orders worship Him (ver. 6) ; creative
Originator of the Universe (ver. 10), such that
the starry depths of space are but the folds of
His vesture, which hereafter He shall change for
another (ver. 12) ; Himself eternal, "the same,"
transcendent above all time, yet all the while
the Son begotten, the Son, infinitely adequate

and infinitely willing to be the final Vehicle of
the Father's voice to us (verses 1, 5, 6). What
is the great truth of Hebrews ii.? Jesus Christ
is MAN. He is other than angelic, for He is God.
But also He is other than angelic, for He is Man
(verses 5, 6, 7). He is the Brother of Man as
truly as He is the Son of God (ver. 11). He has
taken share with us in flesh and blood (ver. 14),
that is to say, He has assumed manhood in that
state or stage in which it is capable of death, and
He has done this on purpose (it is a wonderful thought) that He may be capable of dying.
This blessed Jesus Christ, this God and Man,
our Saviour, was bent upon dying, and that for
a reason altogether connected with us and with
His will to save us (ver. 15). We were immeasurably dear and important to Him. And
our deliverance demanded His identification with
us in nature, and His temptations (ver. 18), and
finally His mysterious suffering. So He came,
He suffered, He was "perfected"—in respect of
capacity to be our Redeemer—"through sufferings" (ver. 10). And now, incarnate, slain, and
risen again, He, still our Brother, is "crowned
with glory and honour" (ver. 9). He is our
Leader (ver. 10). He is our High Priest,
merciful and faithful (ver. 17).

Thus the Epistle, on its way to recall its
readers, at a crisis of confusion and temptation,

to certainty, patience, and peace, leads them—
not last but first—to Jesus Christ. It unfolds
at once to them His glories of Person, His
wonder of Work and Love. It does not elaborately travel up to Him through general con-
siderations. It sets out from Him. It makes
Him the base and reason for all it has to say—
and it has to say many things. Its first theme
is not the Community, but the Lord; not Church
principles, not that great duty of cohesion about
which it will speak, and speak urgently, further
on, but the Lord, in His adorable personal
greatness, in His unique and all-wonderful
personal achievement. To that attitude of
thought it recurs again and again in its later
stages. In one way or another it is always
bidding us look up from even the greatest
related subjects and " consider HIM."

Am I not right in saying that here is a
message straight to the restless heart of our
time, and not least to the special conditions of
Christian life just now in our well-beloved
Church? We must, of course we must, think
about a hundred problems presented by the
circumference of the life of the Christian and
the life of the Church. At all times such
problems, asking for attention and solution,
emerge to every thoughtful disciple's sight. In
our own time they seem to multiply upon one

another with an importunate demand—problems
doctrinal, ritual, governmental, social; the strife
of principles and tendencies within the Church;
all that is involved in the relations between
the Church and the State, and again between the
Church and the world, that is to say, human
life in different or opposed to the living Christian
creed and the spiritual Christian rule.

Well, for these very reasons let us make here
first this brief appeal, prompted by the opening
paragraphs of the great Epistle. If you would
deal aright with the circumference, earnest
Christian of the English Church, live at the
Centre. "Dwell deep." From the Church
come back evermore to Jesus Christ, that from
Jesus Christ you may the better go back to the
Church, bearing the peace and the power of the
Lord Himself upon you.

There is nothing that can serve as a substitute
for this. The "consideration" of our blessed
Redeemer and King is not merely good for us;
it is vital. To "behold His glory," deliberately,
with worship, with worshipping love, *and seen
by direct attention to the mirror of His Word*,
can and must secure for us blessings which we
shall otherwise infallibly lose. This, and this
alone, amidst the strife of tongues and all the
perplexities of life, can develop in us at once
the humblest reverence and the noblest liberty,

convictions firm to resist a whole world in opposition, yet the meekness and the fear which utterly exclude injustice, untruth, hardness, or the bitter word. For us if for any, for us now if ever, this first great message of the Epistle meets a vital need ; " CONSIDER HIM."

2

A Heart of Faith

WE have just endeavoured to find a message, "godly and wholesome, and necessary for these times," in the opening paragraphs in the Epistle to the Hebrews. We come now to interrogate our oracle again, and we open the third chapter as we do so.

Here again we find the Epistle full, first, of "Jesus Christ Himself." He is "the Apostle and the High Priest of our profession" (ver. 1), or let us read rather, "our confession," the "confession" of us who are loyal to His Name as His disciples. We are expressly called here to do what the first two chapters implied that we must do—to "consider Him" (ver. 1), to bend upon His Person, character, and work the attention of the whole heart and mind. We are pointed to His holy fidelity to His mission (ver. 2) in words which equally remind us of His subordination to the Father's will and of His absolute authority as the Father's perfect Representative. We are reminded (ver. 3) of that magnificent other side of His position, that He acts and administers in "the house of God" not as a servant but as the Father's "own SON (ver. 6) that serveth Him." Nay, such is He that the "house" in which He does His filial service is a building which He Himself has reared (ver. 3); He is its Architect and its Constructor in a sense in which none could be who is not Divine. Yes, He is no less than God (ver. 4); God Filial, God so conditioned that He is also the faithful Sent-One of the Father, but none the less GOD. We saw Him already in the first chapter (ver. 10), placed before us in His majesty as the Originator of the material Universe, to whom the starry skies are but His robe, to be put on and put off in season. Here He is the doer of a yet more wonderful achievement; He is the Builder of the Church of the Faithful. For the "house" which He thus built is nothing else than "we" (ver. 6), we who by faith have entered into the structure of the "living stones" (see 1 Pet. ii. 5), and who, by "the confidence and the rejoicing of our hope," abide within it.

Thus the blessed Lord is before us here again, filling our sphere of thought and contemplation. It is here just as it is in the Epistle to the Colossians. There, as here, errors and confusions

in the Church are in view—a subtle theosophy
and also a retrograde ceremonialism, probably
both amalgamating into one dangerous total.
And St. Paul's method of defence for his con-
verts there—what is it? Above all, it is the
presentation of Jesus Christ, in the glories of
His Person and His Work. He places HIM in
the very front of thought, first as the Head,
Founder, and Corner-stone of the Universe;
then as the Head, Redeemer, and Life of the
Church. With HIM so seen he meets the
dreamy thinker and the ceremonial devotee;
Christ is the ultimate and only repose, alike
for thought and for the soul.

In this Epistle as in that we have the same
phenomenon, deeply suggestive and seasonable
for our life to-day. In both cases, not only for
individuals but for the Church, there was mental
and spiritual trouble. Alike in Phrygian Colossæ
and wherever the "Hebrews" lived there was an
invasion of church difficulties and confusion. A
certain affinity in detail links the two cases
together. Colossian Christians and Hebrew
Christians, under widely different circumstances,
and no doubt in very different tones, persuasive
in one case, threatening in the other, were pressed
to *retrograde* from the sublime simplicity and
fulness of the truth. Their danger was what
I may venture to call a certain medievalism.

Not Mosaism, not Prophetism, but Judaism, the successor and distortion of the ancient revelations, invited or commanded their adhesion, or, in the case of the "Hebrews," their return, as to the one true faith and fold. There were great differences in detail. At Colossæ it does not seem that the "medievalists" professed to deny Christianity; rather they professed to teach the Judaistic version of it as the authentic type. Among the "Hebrews" anti-Christianity was using every effort to allure or to alarm the disciples back to open Rabbinism, "doing despite to the Son of God." But both streams of tendency went in the same general direction so far that they put into the utmost prominence aspects of religion full of a traditional ceremonialism, and of the idea of human meritorious achievement rather than of a spiritual reliance for the salvation of the soul.

Deeply significant it is that in both cases we have the danger met thus—by the presentation of the Incarnate Redeemer Himself, in His personal and official glory, to the most immediate possible view of every disciple, "nothing between." The Epistles, both of them, have much to say on deep general principles. But all this they say in vital connexion with Jesus Christ; and about HIM they say most of all. He is the supreme Antidote. He, "considered," considered fully, is

not so much the clue out of the labyrinth as the
great point of view from which the mind and the
soul can look down upon it and see how tortuous,
and also how limited, it is.

But the message of our chapter has not yet
been fully heard. It has spoken to us of Christ
Jesus, and of the "consideration" of Him to
which we are called. At its close it speaks to
us of faith : "Take heed, lest there be in any of
you an evil heart of unbelief, in departing from
the living God" (ver. 12). "To whom sware
He that they should not enter into His rest,
but to them that believed not? So we see that
they could not enter in because of unbelief"
(verses 18, 19).

That is to say, our "consideration" of Jesus
Christ must not be all our action towards Him,
if we would be sure, and safe, and strong. It
must be but the preliminary to a "heart of
faith." That is to say again, we must personally
and practically take Him at His word, and rely
upon Him, committing our souls and our all to
Him, to Him directly, to Him solely. We must,
in the exercise of this reliance, use Him evermore as our Prophet, Priest, and King. We
must venture upon His promises, just as Israel
ought to have ventured upon the promises of
Him who had redeemed them, although He
tried their will and power to do so by the

terrors of the wilderness and by the giants of Canaan.

Thus to rely is faith; for faith is personal confidence in the Lord in His promise. And such faith is not only, as it is, the empty hand which receives Divine blessings in detail. It is the empty arms which clasp always that comprehensive blessing, the presence of "the living God" in Christ, so making sure of a secret of peace, of rest, of decision, of strength, of deep-sighted and tranquil thought upon "things which differ," which is of infinite importance at a time of confusion and debate in the Christian Church.

Therefore, alike for our safety and for our usefulness, let us first afresh "consider Him." And then let us afresh "take heed" that with "a good heart of faith" we draw to and abide in union with the "considered" Christ, in whom we know and possess the living God.

3

Unto Perfection

Hebrews 4-6

OUR study of the great Epistle takes here another step, covering three short but pregnant chapters. So pregnant are they that it would be altogether vain to attempt to deal with them thus briefly were we not mindful of our special point of view. We are pondering the Epistle not for all that it has to say, but for what it has to say of special moment and application for certain needs of our own time.

The outline of the portion before us must accordingly be traced. In detail it presents many questions of connexion and argument, for, particularly in chapter iv., the apostolic thought takes occasionally a parenthetical flight of large circuit. But in outline the progression may be traced without serious difficulty.

We have first the appeal to exercise the promptitude and decision of faith, in view of the magnificent promise of a Canaan of sacred

rest made to the true Israel in Christ. Even
to "seem" (iv. 1) to fail of this, even to seem
to sink into a desert grave of unbelief while
"the rest of faith" is waiting to be entered, is
a thought to "fear." Great indeed are the
promises; "living" and "energetic" is "the
Word" which conveys them.*

That "Word" is piercing as a sword in its
convictions, for it is the vehicle of His mind
and His holiness "with whom is concerned our
discourse" (iv. 13); while yet it is, on its other
side, a "Gospel" indeed (iv. 2), the message of
supreme good, if only it is met with faith by
the convicted soul. Yes, it is a message which
tells of a land of "rest," near and open, fairer
far than the Canaan on which Caleb reported
and from which he and his fellows brought the
great clusters of its golden vines. Passage after
passage of the old Scriptures (iv. 3–9) shows
that *that* Canaan was no finality, no true *ter-
minus* of the purpose of God; another "rest,"
another "day" of entrance and blessing, was
intimated all along. Unbelief forfeited the true
fruition of even the old Canaan for the old
Israel. And now out of that evil has sprung
the glorious good of a more articulate promise
of the new Canaan, the inheritance of rest in

---

* Ch. iv. 12, if I am right, follows in thought upon iv. 2,
leaving a long and deep parenthesis between.

Christ, destined for the new Israel. But as
then, so now, the promise, if it is to come to its
effect, must be met and realized by obedient faith.
Despite all the difficulties, in face of whatever may seem the Anakim of to-day, looking to
Him who is immeasurably more than Moses, and
who is the true and second Joshua,* we must
make haste to enter in by the way of faith.
We must "mingle the word with faith" (iv. 2),
into one glorious issue of attained and abiding
rest. We must lay our hearts soft and open
(iv. 7) before the will of the Promiser. We
must "be in earnest" to enter in (iv. 11).

Then, at iv. 14, the appeal takes us in
beautiful order more directly to Him who is
at once the Leader and the Promised Land.
And again He stands before us as a "great High
Priest." Our Moses, our Joshua, is also our
more than Aaron, combining in Himself every
possible qualification to be our guide and pre-
server as we enter in. He stands before us
in all the alluring and endearing character of
mingled majesty and mercy; a High Priest, a
great High Priest, immeasurably great; He has
"passed through the heavens" (iv. 14) to the
Holiest, to the throne, the celestial mercy-seat
(iv. 16) "within the veil" (vi. 19); He is the
SON (v. 5); He is the Priest-King, the true

* The "Jesus" (iv. 8) of the Authorized Version.

Melchizedek; He is all this for ever (vi. 20).
But on the other hand He is the sinner's
Friend, who has so identified Himself in His
blessed Manhood with the sinner, veritably
taking our veritable nature, that He is "able
to feel with our weaknesses" (iv. 15); "able
to feel a sympathetic tolerance (μετριοπαθεῖν)
towards the ignorant and the wandering" (v. 2);
understanding well "what sore temptations mean,
for He has felt the same"; yea, He has known
what it is to "cry out mightily and shed tears"
(v. 7) in face of a horror of death; to cast Himself as a genuine suppliant, in uttermost suffering,
upon paternal kindness; to get to know by
personal experience what submission means
(ἔμαθε τὴν ὑπακοήν, v. 8); "not my will
but Thine be done."

Such is the "Leader of our faith," so great, so
glorious, so perfect, so tender, so deep in fellowship with us. Shall we not follow Him into
"the rest," though a "Jordan rolls between"
and though cities of giants seem to frown upon
us even on the other side? Shall we not dare
thither to follow HIM out of the desert of our
"own works"?

Much, says the Epistle (v. 11, etc.), is to be
said about Him; the theme is deep, it is in-
exhaustible, for He is God and Man, one Christ.
And the Hebrew believers (and is it not the

same with us ?) are not quick to learn the great
lesson of His glory, and so to grow into the
adult manhood of grace. But let us try ; let us
address ourselves to "bear onwards (φερώμεθα)
to perfection " (vi. 1), in our thought, our faith,
and so in our experience. The great foundation
factors must be for ever there, the initial acts
or attitudes of repentance, and of "faith towards
God "; the abandonment of the service of sin,
including the bondage of a would-be salvation
of self by self, and the simple turning God-ward
of a soul which has come to despair of its own
resources—truths symbolized and sealed by the
primal rites of baptism and blessing (vi. 2); and
then the great revealed facts in prospect, resurrection and judgment, must be always remembered and reckoned with. These however must
be "left" (vi. 1), not in oblivion but in progress,
just as a building "leaves" the level of its
always necessary foundation. We must "bear
onwards" and upwards, into the upper air of
the fulness of the truth of the glory of our
Christ. We must seek "perfection," the profound maturity of the Christian, by a maturer
and yet maturer insight into Him. Awful is
the spiritual risk of any other course. The
soul content to stand still is in peril of a
tremendous fall. To know about salvation at
all, and not to seek to develope the knowledge

towards "perfection," is to expose one's self
to the terrible possibility of the fate reserved
for those who have much light but no love
(vi. 4-9).* But this, by the grace of God, shall
not be for the readers of the Epistle. They
have shewn living proofs of love already,
practical and precious, for the blessed Name's
sake (vi. 10). Only, let them remember the
spiritual law—the necessity of growth, of progress, of "bearing onwards to perfection"; the
tremendous risks of a subtle stagnation; the
looking back; the pillar of salt.

In order that full blessing may thus be theirs,
let them look for it in the only possible direction.
Let them take again to their souls the mighty
promise of eternal benediction (vi. 14), sealed
and crowned with the Promiser's gracious oath
in His own Name, binding Himself to fidelity
under the bond of His own majesty (vi. 13).
Aye, and then let them again "consider" HIM
in whom promise and oath are embodied and
vivified for ever; in whom rests—nay, in whom
consists—our anchor of an eternal hope (vi. 19);
Jesus, our Man of men, our High Priest of the
everlasting order, now entered "within the veil,"

---

* I make no attempt here to expound in detail the formidable
words of vi. 4-8. But I believe that their purport is fairly
described in the sentence above in the text. Their true scrip-
tural illustrations are to be sought in a Balaam and a Judas.

into the place of the covenant and the glory, and
"as Forerunner on our behalf" (vi. 20). To
follow Him in there, in the "consideration" of
faith and of worshipping love—this is the secret,
to the end, for "bearing onwards to perfection."

Our review of the passage is thus in some sort
over. Confessedly it is an outline; but I do not
think that any vital element in the matter has
been overlooked. Much of the message we are
seeking has been inevitably given us by the
way; we may be content now to gather up and
summarize the main result.

The "Hebrews," then, and their special
circumstances of difficulty, are here in view,
as everywhere else in the Epistle. Tempted to
"fall away," to give up the "hope set before
them," to relapse to legalism, to bondage, to the
desert, to a famine of the soul, to barrenness and
death—here they are dealt with, in order to
the more than prevention of the evil. And
here, as ever, the remedy propounded is our
Lord Jesus Christ, in His personal glory, in His
majestic offices, in His unfathomable human
sympathy, seen in perfect harmony of light with
His eternal greatness.

The remedy is Christ; a deeper, fuller, always
maturing sight of Christ. The urgent necessity
is first promptitude and then progress in respect
of knowing Him.

At the risk of a charge of iteration and monotony, I reaffirm that here is the great antidote for the many kindred difficulties of our troubled time. From how many sides comes the strain! Sometimes from that of an open naturalism; sometimes from that of a partial yet far-reaching "naturalism under a veil" which some recent teachings on "The Being of Christianity" may exemplify, with principles and presuppositions which largely underlie the extremer forms, certainly, of the modern critique of Scripture; sometimes from the opposite quarter of an ecclesiasticism which more or less exaggerates or distorts the great ideas of corporate life and sacramental operation. It would be idle to ignore the subtle *nuances* of difference between mind and mind, and the resultant varying incidence in detail of great and many-sided truths. But is it not fair and true to say that, on the whole, the supreme personal glory of Christ, as presented direct to the human soul in its august and ineffable loveliness, in its infinite lovableness, is what alike the naturalistic and the ultra-ecclesiastic theories of religion tend to becloud? On the other side, accordingly, it is in the "consideration" of that glory, in acquaintance with that wonderful Christ, that we shall find the glow which can melt and overcome the cloud.

We must put ourselves continually in face of the revelation of this in the Word of God. We must let that revelation so sink into the heart as to do its self-verifying work there thoroughly, yet with a growth never to be exhausted. We must " bear onwards " evermore " unto perfection "—in " knowing Him." So we shall stand, and live, and love, and labour on.

4

Our Great Melchizedek

Hebrews 7

THERE is a symmetrical dignity all its own in the seventh chapter of the Hebrews. I recollect listening, now many years ago, to a characteristic exposition of it by the late beloved and venerated Edward Hoare, in a well-known drawing-room at Cromer—a "Bible Reading" full alike of mental stimulus and spiritual force. He remarked, among many other things, that the chapter might be described as a sermon, divided under three headings, on the text of Psalm cx. 4. This division and its significance he proceeded to develope. The chapter opens with a preamble, a statement of the unique phenomena which surround, in the narrative of Genesis, the name and person of Melchizedek. Then, starting from the presupposition, to whose truth the Lord Himself is so abundantly a witness, that the Old Testament is alive everywhere with intimations of the Christ, and

remembering that in the Psalm in question a
mysterious import is explicitly assigned to
Melchizedek, the Writer proceeds to his
discourse. Its theme is the primacy of the
priesthood embodied in Melchizedek over that
represented by Aaron, and the bearing of this on
the glory of Him who is proclaimed a priest for
ever after Melchizedek's order. This theme is presented under headings, somewhat as follows. *First*
(verses 4–14), the one priesthood is greater than
the other *in order*. Abraham, bearing the whole
Aaronic hierarchy potentially within him, defers
to Melchizedek as to his greater. Hence, among
other inferences, the sacred Personage who is a
priest for ever after Melchizedek's order, wholly
independent of Levitical limits, must dominate
and must supersede the order of the sons of Aaron
with their inferior status and with their transitory
lives. *Secondly* (verses 15–19), the one priesthood is greater than the other in respect of *the
finality,* the permanence, the everlastingness, of
the greater Priest and of His office. He is what
He is "for ever, on the scale of the power of
indissoluble life." * As such, He is the Priest
not of an introductory and transient "command-
ment" but of that "better hope" which (ver. 19)
has at last "made perfect" the purpose and the
promise, fulfilled the intention of eternal mercy,

* κατὰ δύναμιν ζωῆς ἀκαταλύτου.

and brought us, the people of this great covenant, absolutely nigh to God. *Thirdly* (verses 20, 21), this second aspect of the supremacy of the greater Priesthood is emphasized and solemnized by one further reference to Psalm cx. 4. There the Eternal, looking upon the mysterious Partner of His throne, is heard not to promise only but to *vow*, with an oath unalterable as Himself, that the Priesthood of "His Fellow" shall be everlasting. No such solemnity of affirmation attended Aaron's investiture. There is something greater here, and more immediately Divine. The "covenant" (ver. 22) committed to the administration of One thus sealed with the oath of Heaven must indeed be "better," and cannot but be final; the goal of the eternal purpose.

Then (verses 23–28) the discourse passes into what we may call its epilogue. The thought recurs to the sublime contrast between the pathetic numerousness of the successors of Aaron, "not suffered to continue by reason of death," and the singleness, the "unsuccessional" identity for ever, of the true Melchizedek, who abides eternally. And then, moving to its end, the argument glows and brightens into an "application" to the human heart. We have in JESUS (the Name has now already been pronounced, ver. 22) a Friend, an Intercessor, infinitely and for ever competent to save us, His true Israel. We

have in Him a High Priest supreme in every
attribute of holiness and power, and qualified
for His work of intercession by that sacrifice
of Himself which is at once solitary and all-
sufficient. Behold then the contrast and the
conclusion. To a great Dispensation, the preparatory, succeeds a greater, the greatest, the
other's end and crown. To the "weak" mortal
priesthood of the law, never warranted by the
vow of God to abide always in possession,
succeeds One who is Priest, and King, and SON,
sealed for His office by the irrevocable vow,
"consecrated for evermore."

Such on the whole, as I recall it, was the
exposition of my venerable friend, in 1887.
Each new reading of the chapter seems to me
to bear out the substantial accuracy of it;
indeed the symmetry and order of the chapter
make it almost inevitable that some such line
should be taken by the explanation. Thus then
it lies before us. It is filled in all its parts
with Jesus Christ, in His character of the true
Melchizedek, our final, everlasting, perfect,
supreme, Divine High Priest.

This simple treatise is not the place for
critical discussions. I do not attempt a formal
vindication of the mystical and Messianic reference of Psalm cx. All I can do here, and
perhaps all I should do, is to affirm solemnly my

belief in it, at the feet of Christ. I am perfectly aware that now, within the Church, and by men unquestionably Christian as well as learned, our Lord's own interpretation of that Psalm,* involving as it does His assertion of its Davidic authorship, is treated as quite open to criticism and disproof. One such scholar does not hesitate to say that, if the majority of modern experts are right as to the non-Davidic authorship, and he seems to think that they are, "our Lord's argument breaks down." All I would remark upon such utterances, coming from men who all the while sincerely adore Christ as their Lord and God, is that they must surely open the way towards conceptions of His whole teaching which make for the ruin of faith. For the question is not at all whether our Redeemer consented to submit to limits in His conscious human knowledge; I for one hold that He assuredly did so. It is whether He consented to that sort of limitation which alone, in respect of imperfection of knowledge, is the real peril of a teacher, and which is his fatal peril—the ignorance of his own ignorance, and a consequent claim to teach where he does not know. In human schools the betrayal of *that* sort of ignorance is a death-blow to confidence, not only in some special utterance, but in the teacher, for it strikes at

* Matt. xxii. 44 ; Luke xx. 42. Cp. Acts ii. 34.

his claim not to knowledge so much as to wisdom, to balance and insight of thought. I venture to say that recent drifts of speculation shew how rapidly the conception of a fallible Christ developes towards that of a wholly imperfect and untrustworthy Christ. And, looking again at the vast phenomenon of the Portrait in the Gospels, I hold that the line of thought which offers by very far the least difficulty, not to faith only but to reason, is that which relies absolutely on His affirmations wherever He is pleased actually to affirm.

So thinking, I take His exposition of Psalm cx. as for me final. And that exposition guarantees at once a typical mystery latent in Gen. xiv. and the rightness of its development in the passage here before us.

But now, what "message" has our chapter for us, in view of the needs of our own time?

First, as to its sacerdotal doctrine. It throws a broad illumination on the grand finality and uniqueness of the mediatorial priesthood of our Lord, the Son of God. It puts into the most vivid possible contrast the age of "the law" and that of Christ as to the priestly conception and institution. Somehow, under the law, there was a need for priests who were "men, having infirmity." For certain grave purposes (not for all, by any means, even in that legal period) it

was the will of God that they should stand
between His Israel and Him.   But the argument
of this chapter, unless it elaborately veils its
true self in clouds, goes directly to shew that
such properly mediatorial functions, in the age of
Christ, are for ever withdrawn from " men, having
infirmity."   Where they stood of old, one after
another, sacrificing, interceding, going in behind
the veil, permitted to draw nearer to God, in an
official sanctity, than their brethren, there now
stands Another, sublime, supreme, alone.   He is
Man indeed, but He is not "man having
infirmity."   He is higher than the heavens,
while He is one with us.   And now our one
secret for a complete approach to God is to
come to God "through HIM."   And this, unless
the chapter is an elaborate semblance of what
it is not, means nothing if it does not mean
that between the Church, and between the soul,
and the Lord Jesus Christ, there is to come
absolutely nothing mediatorial.   As little as the
Jew, for ceremonial purposes, needed an intermediary in dealing with his mortal priest so
little do we, for the whole needs of our being,
need an intermediary in dealing with our eternal
Priest.

In the age of Christ, no office can for one
moment put one " man having infirmity " nearer
to God than another, if this chapter means what

it says. Mediatorial priesthood, a very different thing from commissioned pastorate, has no place in apostolic Christianity, with the vast exception of its sublime and solitary place in the Person of our most blessed Lord.

Then further, the chapter, far from giving us merely the cold gift (as it would be if this were all) of a negative certainty against unlawful human claims, gives us, as its true, its inmost message, a glorious positive. It gives us the certainty that, for every human heart which asks for God, this wonderful Christ, personal, eternal, human, Divine, is quite immediately accessible. The hands of need and trust have but to be lifted, and they hold HIM. And He is the SON. In Him we have the FATHER. We do indeed "*draw nigh* to God through Him."

Therefore we will do it. The thousand confusions of our time shall only make this Divine simplicity the more precious to us. We will at once and continually take Jesus Christ for granted in all the fulness and splendour of His High-priesthood after the order of Melchizedek. That Priesthood is for ever what it is; it is as new and young to-day in its virtue as if the oath had but to-day been spoken, and He had but to-day sat down at the right hand.

Happy we if we use Him thus. He blesses

those who do so with blessings which they cannot analyse, but which they know. Many years ago a Christian lady, daughter of a saintly Nonconformist pastor in the west of Dorset, told me how, in a then distant time, her father had striven to teach a sick man, a young gipsy in a wandering camp, to read, and to come to Christ. The camp moved after a while, and the young man, dying of consumption, took a Bible with him. Time rolled on, and one day a gray-haired gipsy came to the minister's door; it was the youth's father, with the news of his son's happy death, and with his Bible. "Sir, I cannot read a word; but *he* was always reading it, and he marked what he liked with a stick from the fire. And he said you would find one place marked with two lines; it was everything to my poor lad." The leaves were turned, and the stick was found to have scored two lines at the side of Heb. vii. 25 : "He is able also to save them to the uttermost that come unto God by Him, seeing that He ever liveth to make intercession for them."

5

The Better Covenant

THE Person and greatness of our High Priest
are now full before the readers of the
Epistle. The paragraph we enter next, after
one more deliberate contemplation of His
dignity and His qualifications, proceeds to expound His relation to the better and eternal
Covenant. We shall find here also messages
appropriate to our time.

The first step then is a review, a summing up,
a "look again" upon the true King of Righteousness and peace (verses 1, 2). "Such a
High Priest *we have*." It is a wonderful affirmation, not only of His existence but of His
relation to "us," His people. "*We have*" Him.
He has taken His seat indeed "at the right
hand of the throne of the majesty in the
heavens." But this great exaltation has not
removed Him for a moment out of our possession ; we have Him. He is now the great

Minister, the supreme sacerdotal Functionary,
of the heavenly sanctuary, "the true tabernacle," τῆς σκηνῆς τῆς ἀληθινῆς, the non-figura-
tive reality of which the Mosaic structure was
only the shadow; the true scene of unveiled
Presence and immortal worship, "pitched" by
Him whose face makes Heaven, and makes it all
one temple. But this sublimity of our Priest's
place and power does not make Him in the
least less ours; we have Him.

The words invite us to a new and deliberate
look upward, and then to a recollection deeper
than ever that He is held spiritually in our
very hands; that He is a possession, nearer to
us than any other.

Then (verses 3 and following) the thought
moves towards the sacrificial and offertorial
qualifications of this great and most sacred
Person. He is what He is, our High Priest,
our Minister of the sanctuary above, on perfectly
valid grounds. For He is, what every sacerdotal
minister must be, an Offerer. And He is this
in a sense, in a way, congruous to His heavenly
position. He has no blood of goats and
calves to present, like the priests on earth.
Indeed, were He "on earth" (ver. 4), this
greatest of all High Priests "would not even be
a priest" (οὐδ᾽ ἂν ἦν ἱερεύς), an ordinary priest.
For that function, says the Writer, is already filled,

"according to the law," by the Aaronic order, to which He never belonged and never could belong (see vii. 13, 14). It is in charge of the sacred servants (λατρεύουσιν) of the earthly sanctuary, the God-given type and shadow (ver. 5) of the realities of Heaven, but no more than their type and shadow, partial and transient. No, His sacerdotal qualification is of another sort and a greater. What it is which " He hath to offer " in the celestial Holiest is not yet explicitly said ; that is reserved for the ninth chapter, to which this is but the vestibule. But already the Epistle emphasizes the truth that " He *hath somewhat* to offer," so that we may fully realize the completeness of His high-priestly power.

It may be well to pause here, and to ask whether this passage reveals that our Lord Jesus Christ is at this moment " offering " for us, in His heavenly life. We are all aware that this has been widely held and earnestly pressed, sometimes into inferences which, as far as I can see, cannot at all be borne even by the doctrine that He *is* offering for us now. In particular it is said that, if He in glory is offering for His Church, then His Church must, in some sense, as in a counterpart, be offering here on earth, in union with Him. In short, there must still be priests on earth who are ministers of " the example and shadow of heavenly things." But surely, if this Epistle makes anything clear, it makes it clear that our great Priest is the superseding fulfilment of all such ministrations done by "men having infirmity." It is His glory, and it is ours, that He is known by us as our one and all-sufficient Offerer and Mediator. It is precisely as such that "we have Him," in a way to distinguish our position and privilege in a magnificent sense from that of those who needed the sacerdotal aid of their mortal brethren.

But then further, does this passage really intimate at all that He is offering now? The thought appears to be decisively negatived by the grandeur of the terms of the first verse of this chapter. Where, in the heavenly sanctuary, is our High Priest now? He has "taken His seat on the right hand of the throne of the majesty." But enthronement is a thought out of line with the act and attitude of oblation. The offerer stands before the Power he approaches. Our Priest is seated—where Deity alone can sit.

Does not this tell us that the words (ver. 3), "It is necessary that He too should have something to offer," are to be explained not of a continuous historical procedure (to which idea, by the way, the aorist verb προσενέγκῃ would hardly be appropriate), but as the statement of a principle in terms of time? The "necessity" is, not that He should have something to offer now, and to-morrow, and always, but that the matter and act of offering should belong to Him. And they do so belong, in principle and effect, for priestly purposes, by having been once and for ever handled and performed by Him. His "need" is, not to be always offering, but to be always an Offerer. He meets that need by being for ever the Priest who had Himself to offer, and who offered Himself, and who now dispenses from His sacerdotal seat the benedictions based upon the sacrifice of which He is for ever the once accepted Offerer.

Only thus viewed, I venture to say, can this phrase be read in its full harmony with the whole Epistle. "He hath somewhat to offer," in the sense that He has for ever the grand sacerdotal qualification of being an Offerer who, having executed that function, now bears to all eternity its *character*. But He is not therefore always executing the function. Otherwise He must descend from His throne. But His enthronement, His session, is a fact of His present position as important and characteristic as possible in this whole Epistle.

Aaron was not always offering. But he was always an offerer. On the morrow of the Atonement Day he was as much an offerer as on the day itself. All through the year, even until the next Atonement, he was still an offerer. He exercised his priestly functions at all times because, in principle, he " had somewhat to offer " in its proper time. *Our* High Priest knows only one Atonement Day, and it is over for ever. And His Israel have it for their privilege and glory not to be " serving unto an example and shadow " of even His work and office, but to be going always, daily and hourly, direct to Him in His perfect Priesthood, in which they always " have " Him, and to be always abiding, in virtue of Him, " boldly," " with confidence," in the very presence of the Lord.

Then the chapter moves forward (verses 6 and following) to consider the relation between our High Priest and *the Covenant* of which He is the Mediator. Here begins one of the great themes of the Epistle. It will recur again and again, till at last we read (xiii. 20) of " the blood of the Covenant eternal."

This pregnant subject is introduced by a solemn reference to the " promises upon which has been legislated," legally insituted, νενομοθετήται, this new compact between God and man. The reference is to the thirtieth chapter of Jeremiah, from which an extract is here made at length. There the prophet, in the name of his God, explicitly foretells the advent of what we may

reverently call a new departure in the revealed
relations between Jehovah and His people. At
Sinai He had engaged to bless them, yet under
conditions which left them to discover the total
inability of their own sin-stricken wills to meet
His holy while benignant will. They failed, they
broke the pact, and judgment followed them of
course. But now another order is to be taken.
Their King and Lawgiver, without for one
moment ceasing to be such, will also undertake
another function, wholly new, as regards the
method of covenant. He will place Himself so
upon their side as Himself to readjust and
empower their affections and their wills. He
"will put His laws into their mind and write
them upon their hearts," and "they shall all
know Him," with the knowledge which is life
eternal. And further, as the antecedent to all
this, in order to open the path to it, to place
them where this wonderful blessing can rightly
reach and fill them, their King and Lawgiver
pledges Himself to a *previous* pardon, full and
unreserved ; "Their sins and their iniquities
I will remember no more." They shall be set
before Him in an acceptance as full as if they
had never fallen. And then, not as the condition
to this but as the sequel to it, He will so deal
with them, internally and spiritually, that they
shall will His will and live His law. There shall

be no mechanical compulsion; "their mind," "their hearts," full as ever of personality and volition, shall be the matter acted upon. But there shall be a gracious and prevailing influence, deciding their spiritual action along its one true line; "I will put," "I will write."

This is the new, the better, the everlasting Covenant. It is placed here in the largest and most decisive contrast over against the old covenant, the compact of Sinai, "written and engraven in stones" (2 Cor. iii. 7). That compact had done its mysterious work, in convincing man of his sinful incapacity to meet the will of God. Now emerges its wonderful antithesis, in which man is first entirely pardoned, with a pardon which means acceptance, peace, re-instatement into the home and family of God, and then and therefore is internally transfigured by his Father's power into a being who loves his Father's law.

What the prophet foretold was claimed by the Lord Christ Himself, as fulfilled in His Person and His work, when He took the cup of blessing, at the feast of the new Passover of the new Israel, and said, "This cup is the new covenant in my blood." And what He so claimed His great apostle rejoiced in, when he wrote to Corinth (2 iii. 6, etc.) of the "ministry of the new covenant," the covenant of the Spirit, of life, of glory. And here the same truth is

stated again, and in strong connexion again with
Him who is at once its Sacrifice, its Surety, its
Mediator; the Cause, and Guardian, and Giver
of all its blessings. He is such that it is such;
ours is "*so great* a salvation," because of so great
and wonderful a High Priest, the possessor in
very deed of "somewhat to offer," and now, with
hands full of the fruits of that offering, "seated"
for us "on the right hand of the throne of the
majesty in the heavens."

Here is a message for our times, in a sense
which seems to me special, pressing, and deeply
beneficent. For the terms of that new covenant
are nothing less than the glorious essence, the
Divine peculiarity, of the Gospel of the grace of
God. This forgiveness, this most sincere and
entirely unearned amnesty, this oblivion of the
sins of the people of God—do we hear very
much about it now, even where by tradition it
might be most expected? But do we not need
it now? Was there ever a time when human
hearts would be more settled and more energized
than now, amidst their moral restlessness, by a
wise, thoughtful, but perfectly unmistakable re-
affirmation of the sublime fulness of Divine
forgiveness in Christ? Men may think that
they can do without that message. They may
bid us throw the whole weight of preaching upon
self-sacrifice, upon social service, upon conduct at

large. But the fully wakeful soul knows that it is only then capacitated for self-sacrifice in the Lord's footsteps when it has received the warrant of forgiveness, written large in His sacred blood, finding pardon and peace at the foot of His sacrificial Cross. Then turn to the second limb of the covenant, a limb greater even than the first, inasmuch as for it the first is provided and guaranteed. Do we hear too much about this covenant blessing now? Do our pulpits too frequently and too fully give out the affirmation that God in Christ stands pledged and covenanted to work the moral transfiguration of His believing Israel, to act so on "the first springs of thought and will" that our being shall freely respond to His free action upon it, and will His will, and live His law? But was there ever greater need for such an affirmation than in our time, so restless, so unsatisfied, and, deep below all its superficial arrogance, so disappointed, so discouraged?

Let us return upon the rich treasures of this great Compact of God in Christ. The Covenant is ever new, for it is eternal. And it lies safe in the ministering hands of Him who died to inaugurate it and make it good, and who lives to shower its blessings down. He is on the right hand of the throne of the majesty in the heavens. And " *we have* " Him.

6

Sanctuary and Sacrifice

Hebrews 9

THE Epistle has exhibited to us the glory of the
eternal Priest and the wealth and grandeur
of the new Covenant. It advances now towards
the Sanctuary and the Sacrifice wherein we see
that covenant sanctified and sealed, under the
auspices of our great " Priest upon His throne."

The Teacher first dilates to the Hebrews
upon the outstanding features of the type. He
enumerates the main features of that " sanctuary,
adapted to this (visible) world" (τὸ ἅγιον,
κοσμικόν), which was attached to the first
covenant (ver. 1).* Particularly, he emphasizes
its double structure, which presented first a
consecrated chamber, holy but not holiest, the
depository of lamp and table, but then beyond
it, parted from it by the inner curtain, the
adytum itself, the Holiest Place, where lay ready

* Assuredly we must delete σκηνή from the text in this verse,
and understand διαθήκη (see viii. 13) after ἡ πρώτη.

42

for use "a golden censer," the vessel needful for the making of the incense-cloud which should veil the glory, and, above all, the Ark of that first covenant of which so much has now been said. There it lay, with the manna and the budding rod, symbols of Mosaic and Aaronic power and function; and the tablets of that law which was written not on the heart but on the stone; and the mercy-seat above them, and the cherubic bearers of the Shechinah above the mercy-seat; symbols of a reconciliation and an access yet to be revealed (verses 2–5).

Such was the sanctuary, as depicted to the mind of the believing Hebrew in the books which he almost worshipped as the oracles of God. That tabernacle he had never seen; that ark he knew had long vanished out of sight. The temple of Herod, with its vacant Holiest, was the sanctuary of his generation. But the Mosaic picture of the Tent and of the Ark was for him the abiding standard, the Divine ideal, the pattern of the realities in the heavens; and to it accordingly the Epistle directs his thought, as it prepares to display those realities before him.*

* I do not attempt in these papers to do more than allude to the controversy of our time over the historical character of the Mosaic books. But I must allude in passing to a noteworthy German critique of the Wellhausen theory, "by a former adherent," W. Möller: *Bedenken gegen die Graf-Wellhausensche Hypothese, von einem früheren Anhänger*

Then it proceeds to a similar presentation of
one great feature in the ritual, the "praxis,"
connected with this Tent of Sanctuaries. It
takes the reader to his Book of Leviticus, and
to its order of Atonement. There (ch. xvi.)
a profound emphasis is laid upon both the
secluded sanctity of the inner shrine, the place
of the Presence, and the sacrificial process by
which alone the rare privilege of entrance into
it could be obtained. The outer chamber was
the daily scene of priestly ministration. But
the inner was, officially at least, entered once
only in the year, and by the High Priest alone,
in the solitary dignity of his office. And even
he went in there only as bearing in his very
hands the blood of immolated victims, blood
which he offered, presented, in the Holiest, with
an express view to the Divine amnesty for
another year's tale of "ignorances" (ἀγνοήματα,
ver. 7), his own and the people's.

Such was the sanctuary, such the atoning
ritual, attached to the first covenant. All was
"mysteriously meant," with a significance in-

(Gütersloh, 1899). The writer, a young and vigorous student
and thinker, explains with remarkable force the immense
difficulties from the purely critical point of view in the way
of the theory that the account of the Tabernacle was invented
by "Levitistic" leaders of the time of the Captivity. The
work has been translated into English, and published by the
Religious Tract Society "*Are the Critics right?*"

finitely deeper than what any thought of Moses,
or of Ezra, could of itself have given it. "The
Holy Ghost intimated" (ver. 8), through that
guarded shrine and those solitary, seldom-granted,
death-conditioned entrances into it, things of
uttermost moment for the soul of man. There
stood the Tent, there went in the lonely Priest,
with the blood of bull and goat, as "a parable
for the period now present," * the time of the
Writer and his readers, in which a ritual of
offering was still maintained whose annual re-
currence proved its inadequacy, its non-finality.
Yes, this majestic but sombre system pictured
a state of jealous reserve between the worshippers and their God. Its propitiations were of
a kind which, in the nature of things, could not
properly and in the way of virtual force set the
conscience free from the sense of guilt, "per-
fecting the worshipper conscience-wise." They
could only "sanctify with a view to the purity
of the flesh" (ver. 13), satisfying the conditions
of a national and temporal acceptance. Its
holiest place was indeed approachable, once
annually, by one representative person; enough

* I think the Revisers are right in giving "*now* present"
instead of "*then* present" as the rendering for τὸν ἐνεστηκότα
(ver. 9). The Epistle alludes, so I should conjecture, to the
period of its writing as a time when the sacrifices were still going
on, albeit on the eve of cessation.—It seems best to read καθ᾽ ἥν,
not καθ᾽ ὅν, in ver. 9 : "in accordance with which *parable*."

to illustrate and to seal a hope; but otherwise,
and far more deeply, the conditions symbolized
separation and a Divine reserve. But "the good
things to come"* were in the Divine view all
along. The "time of reformation" (ver. 10),
of the rectification of the failures suffered under
the first covenant, drew near. Behold Messiah
steps upon the scene, the true High Priest
(ver. 11). Victim and Sacrificer at once, He
sheds His own sacrificial blood (ver. 12) on
the altar of Golgotha, to be His means (διὰ
c. gen.) of acceptable approach. And then He
passes, through the avenue of a sanctuary "not
made with hands" (ver. 11), even the heavenly
world itself (cp. διεληλυθότα τοὺς οὐρανούς,
iv. 14), into the Holiest Place of the eternal
Presence on the throne. He goes in thither,
there to be, and there to do, all that we know
of from the long context previous to this chapter,
even to sit down accepted at the right hand of
the majesty on high, King of Righteousness and
Peace. And this action and entrance is, in its
very nature, a thing done once and for ever.
The true High Priest, being what He is, doing
what He has done, has indeed "found *eternal*
redemption for us" (ver. 12). It is infinitely

---

* Possibly we should read τῶν γενομένων ἀγαθῶν, "the good
things that are come" (R.V. marg.). But the practical difference is not great.

unnecessary now to imagine a *repetition* of sacrifice, entrance, offering, acceptance, for Him, and for us in Him. Such an Oblation, the self-offering of the Incarnate Son in the power of the Eternal Spirit (ver. 14), what can it not do for the believing worshipper's welcome in, and his perfect peace in the assurance of the covenanted love of God? Is it not adequate to "purge the conscience from dead works," to lift from it, that is to say, the death-load of unforgiven transgressions, and to lead the Christian in, as one with his atoning Lord, " to serve a living God," with the happy service of a worshipper (λατρεύειν) who need "go no more out" from the Holy Place of peace?

But the Teacher has not yet done with the wealth of the Mosaic types of our full salvation. He has more to say about the profound truth that the New Covenant needed for its Mediator, its Herald, its Guarantor and Conveyer of blessing, not a Moses but a Messiah, who could both die and reign, could at once be Sacrifice and Priest. Covenants, in the normal order of God's will in Scripture, demanded death for their ratification. "Where covenant is, there must be brought in the death of the covenant-victim." * So it was

---

* So, with the late Professor Scholefield (*Hints on a New Translation*) I venture to render τοῦ διαθεμένου. I am convinced that this rendering, though it has the serious difficulty of lacking any clear parallel to certify the application of διαθεμένου, is necessitated by the connexion.

with the old covenant (verses 18–21) in the
narrative of Exodus xxiv. So, throughout the
Mosaic rules, we find "remission," practically
always, conditioned by "blood-shedding" (ver.
22). Peace with violated holiness was to be
attained only by means of sacrificial death.
The terrestrial sanctuary, viewed as polluted
by the transgressions of the worshippers who
sought its benefits, required sacrificial death, the
blood of bulls and goats, so to "cleanse" it that
God could meet Israel there in peace (ver. 23).
Even so, only after a higher and holier order,
must it be with the better covenant and that
invisible sanctuary where a reconciled God may
for ever meet in peace His spiritual Israel.
There must be priestly immolation and an
offered sacrifice; there must be peace conditioned by life-blood shed. And such is the
work of our Messiah-Priest. He has "borne
the sins of many" (ver. 28). Presenting Himself (ver. 6) as the Atonement Victim, in the
heavenly Holiest, He has thereby "borne,"
uplifted (ἀνενεγκεῖν), in that Presence, for
pardon and peace, the sins of the new Israel.
And so "the heavenly things" are, relatively
to that Israel, "cleansed"; their God can meet
them in that sanctuary with an intimacy and
access free and perfect, because their High
Priest and Mediator has done His work for

them. For ever and ever now they need no
new *sacrifice*; His blood, once shed, is eternally
sufficient. Aye, and they need now for ever no
repeated *offering* (ver. 25) of sacrifice, no new
presentation of His blood before the throne, since
once He has taken His place upon it. To offer
again He must suffer again (ver. 26). For it is
the law of His office first to offer—*and then to
take His place at the right hand.* He must leave
that place, He must descend again to a cross, if
He is to take again the attitude of presentation.
"Henceforth" He sits, "expecting" (see below,
x. 13), "till His enemies be made His footstool."
And His Israel on their part wait (ver. 28),
"expecting," till in that bright promised day
"He appears, the second time, without sin," un-
encumbered by the burthen He once carried for
them, "unto salvation," the salvation which means
the final glory. "Once, only once"—this is the
sublime law of that Sacrifice and that Offering.
As death for us men comes "once," and then
there follows "judgment," so the death of Christ,
the "offering" of Christ, comes "once," and then
comes, in a wonderful paradox, not judgment but
"salvation," for them that are found in Him.

The messages of this chapter for our time
are equally manifest and weighty. It closes
with the assertion of a principle which should
be for all time decisive against all sorts and

forms of "re-presentation" of the Lord our
Sacrifice. He has "offered" Himself once and
for ever, and is now, on our behalf, not in the
Presence only but upon the Throne. Yet more
urgent, more vital, if possible, is the affirmation
here of the need and of the virtue of His
vicarious death. The chapter puts His blood-
shedding before us in a way as remote as
possible from a mere example, or from a
suffering meant to do its work mainly by a
mysterious impartation to us of the power to
suffer. He dies "for the redemption of the
transgressions under the first covenant"—in
other words, for the welcome back to God of
those who had sinned against His awful Law.
He dies that we, "the called," "might receive
the promise of an eternal inheritance." He dies,
He offers, that we, wholly and solely because He
has done so, may find the heavenly, invisible,
spiritual Holiest a place of perfect peace with
God, dwelling in it as in our spirits' home.

Are these the characteristic accents of the
voice of the modern Church? Have we not
need to listen again, reverent and believing,
to the ninth chapter of the Hebrews, as it
discourses about sanctuary, and sacrifice, and
offering, and peace?

7

Full, Perfect, and Sufficient

Hebrews 10

THE heaven-taught Teacher has led us now along the avenue of the Levitical foreshadowings, through the prophetic symbolism of the old high-priesthood, through the holy place and the holiest. The pathway, marked by the blood of animal sacrifices, hallowing the awful terms of the covenant of works, has brought us to the true Tabernacle and true Sacrifice, to the better and final Covenant, to the supreme High Priest. The teaching has left us, as the ninth chapter closes, " looking up steadfastly into heaven," recollecting where the Lord is and why He is there ; thinking how we, His Israel, " have Him " for our Representative and Mediator as He "appears in the presence of God for us," and expecting the hour of joy and glory when He will put aside the curtains of that tabernacle, and come forth to crown us with the final benediction, receiving us " unto the salvation " of eternity (ix. 27, 28).

It is a solemn but a happy attitude. It can be taken by those only who have "fled for refuge to the hope set before them." But they are to take it, as those who feel beneath their feet the rock of an assured salvation and know their open way to the heart of God.

The argument now proceeds in living continuity. Its business now is to accentuate and develope the supremacy, the ultimacy—if the word may be allowed—of the finished work of the true High Priest, in contrast to the provisional and preparatory "law." The Writer has said much to us in this way before, particularly in the preceding three chapters of the Epistle. But he must emphasize it again, for it is the inmost purport of his whole discourse. And he must do it now with the urgency of one who has in view a real peril of apostasy. His readers are hard pressed, by persuasions and by terrors, to turn back from Christ to the Judaistic travesty of the message of the Law. He must tell them not only of the splendour of Messiah's work but of the absolute finality of it for man's salvation. To forsake it is to "forsake their own mercy," to "turn back into perdition."

So he begins with a reminder of the incapacity of the Law to save, by pointing to the ceaseless *repetition* of the sacrificial acts. Year by year, on one Atonement Day after another, the blood-shedding, the blood-sprinkling, the propitiation, had to be done again. Year by year accordingly the worshippers were treated as "not perfect" (ver. 1); that is to say, in the clear light of the context, they were not perfect as to reconciliation, they were loaded still with the burthen of guilt. The "conscience of sins" (ver. 2) haunted them still, that is to say, the weary sense of an unsettled score of offences, a position precarious and unassured before the Judge.

We believe—nay, with the Psalms in our hands, such Psalms as xxiii., and xxxii., and ciii., we know—that for the really contrite and loyal heart, even under the Law, there were large experiences of peace and joy. But these blessings were not due to the sacrifices of the tabernacle or the temple, however divinely ordered. They were due to revelations from many quarters of the character of the Lord Jehovah, and not least, assuredly, to the conviction—how could the more deeply taught souls have helped it? — that this vast and death-dealing ceremonial had *a goal* which alone could explain it, in some transcendent climax of remission. But in itself the ritual emphasized not gladness but judgment, not love but the dread fact of guilt. And the blood of goats could not for a moment be thought of (ver. 4) as *by itself* able to make peace with God. At best it laid stress on the need of something which, while analogous to it on one side, should be transcendently different and greater on the other.

The priests daily (ver. 11), the high priest yearly, as they slew and burnt the victims, and sprinkled blood, and wafted incense, in view of Israel's tale of offences against his King, were all, by their every action, prophets of that mysterious something yet to come. They "made remembrance of sins" (ver. 3), writing always anew upon the conscience of the worshipper the certainty that sin, in its form of guilt, is a tremendous reality in the court of God, that it calls importunately for propitiation, while yet animal propitiations can never, by their very nature, be really propitiatory of themselves. Yet the God of Israel had commanded them; they could not be *mere* forms therefore. What could they be then but types and suggestions of a reality which should at last justify the symbolism by a victorious fulfilment? Thus was an oracle like Isa. liii. made possible. And thus, as we are taught expressly here (verses 5–7), the oracle of Psalm xl. was made possible, in which "sacrifices and offerings," though prescribed to Israel by his King, were not "delighted in" by Him, not "willed" by Him for their own sake at all, but in which

One speaks to the Eternal about another and supreme immolation, for which He who speaks "has come" to present HIMSELF. "Ears hast Thou opened for me," runs the Hebrew (Ps. xl. 6). "A body hast Thou adjusted for me," was the Greek paraphrase of the Seventy, followed by the holy Writer here. It was as if the paraphrasts, looking onward to the Hope of Israel, would interpret and expand the thought of an uttermost *obedience*, signified by the *ear*, into the completer thought of the *body* of which the listening ear was part, and which should be given up wholly in sacrifice to God.*

If this is at all the course of the Writer's exposition, there is nothing arbitrary in the sequel to it. He explains the enigmatic Psalm by finding in it the crucified and self-offering High Priest of our profession. Of Him "the roll of the book" had spoken, as the supreme doer and bearer for us of the will of God. His sacred Body was the Thing indicated by the prophetic altars of Aaron. When He "offered" it, presenting it to the eternal Holiness on our behalf, when He let it be done to death because we had sinned, so that we might be accepted because it, because He, had suffered—then did He "fill" the types

---

* So Kay, on this passage, in the *Speaker's Commentary*.

"full" of their true meaning, and so close their work for ever.

Yes, that work was now *for ever* closed by the attainment of its goal. Moreover, *His* work of sacrifice and of offering, of suffering and of presentation, was for ever finished also. This is the burthen and message of the whole passage (verses 11–18). "Once for all" (ἐφάπαξ), "once for ever," the holy Body has been offered (ver. 10). "He offered one sacrifice for sins in perpetuity," εἰς τὸ διηνεκές (ver. 12). And therefore, not only for the priests of the old rite but for the High Priest of the heavenly order, "there is no more offering for sin" (ver. 18).

And why? Because, for the new Israel, for the chosen people of faith (ver. 39), the supreme sacrifice and offering has done its work. It has "sanctified" them (verses 10, 29); that is to say, it has hallowed them into God's accepted possession by its reconciling and redeeming efficacy. For its virtue does much more than rescue; it annexes and appropriates what it saves. It has "perfected" them (ver. 14); that is to say, it has placed them effectually in that position of complete "peace with God" which guilt while still unsettled makes impossible. It has "put them among the children," within the home circle of Divine love. It has done this "in perpetuity," εἰς τὸ διηνεκές (ver. 14); that is to say, they will never to the very last need anything but that sacrifice and offering to be the cause and the warrant of their place within that home. "Their sins and their iniquities" their reconciled Father "will never remember any more" against them (ver. 17), in the sense that the sacrifice once presented on their behalf will be before Him every moment in the person of the Self-Sacrificer, who sits beside Him, "appearing for us." They are the Israel of the great New Covenant. And that covenant, as we have already remembered (viii. 7–13), provides for the spiritual transformation of the wills of the covenanters; the law of their God shall be "written on" their very minds; that is to say, they shall will His will as their own. But such a "writing" demands, by the very nature of things, that *first, not last*, there should be an absolute remission. For without remission there could not be inward peace, nor therefore filial and paternal harmony. So, for this deep mass of reasons, the new Israelites are *first* wholly accepted for the sake of their self-offered High Priest, that *then* they may be wholly transformed by His power, working through His peace, within themselves.

The great closing paragraphs of the chapter (verses 19–39) are one long application of this

sublime finality of the one Offering and this pre-
sentness of our complete acceptance. First, the
new Israelite, his " heart sprinkled from an evil
conscience " (ver. 22), released, that is to say, by
the applied Sacrifice from the haunting sense of
guilt, and having his " body washed with pure
water," the baptismal sign and seal of the
covenant blessing, is *to behave as what he is*—
the child at home. That home is the Holy
Place ; it is the very Presence of his God ; but
it is home. He is to pass into that sanctuary,
along the pathway traced by the blessed blood,
not hesitating, but with the " boldness " of an
absolute reliance, perfectly free while perfectly
and wonderingly humbled ; " with a true heart,
in fulness, in full assurance, of faith " (ver. 22).
He is to hold fast his avowal of assurance, and
meanwhile he is to animate the brethren round
him to a holy rivalry (ver. 24) of love and
zeal. He is to maintain all possible worshipping
union with them, in the dawning light of the
promised return of the now enthroned High
Priest (ver. 25).

Then, further, the new Israelite is to cherish
the grace of godly fear. The " boldness " of the
loyal child is to go along with the clear recollection that outside the holy home there lies only
" a wilderness of woe." To leave it, to turn back
from it, to be a renegade from covenant joys,

is no mere exchange of the best for the less good. It means multiplied and capital rebellion. No legal shadow-sacrifices will shelter now the soul that forsakes the eternal High Priest and casts His Self-Sacrifice aside. To do that is to set out towards a hopeless retribution, towards the fire of judgment, the vengeance of the living God (verses 26–31).

With tender urgency he pleads for fresh memories and fresh resolves (verses 32–35). He recalls to them days, not long ago, when they had borne shame and loss, "a conflict of sufferings," fellowship with outcast and imprisoned saints, spoiling of their own possessions —all made more than bearable by the joy of their wonderful "enlightenment" (ver. 32). Let them do so still, in full view of the coming crown. Let them grasp afresh the glorious privilege of "boldness" (ver. 35), reaffirming to themselves with strong assurance that they are "sanctified," "perfected," at home with God in Christ. Let them rise up and go on in that noble "patience" (ver. 36) which "suffers and is strong." It is only "a very little while" before the High Priest will reappear. And the "faith" which takes Him at His word will, as the prophet witnesses (Hab. ii. 4), bridge that little while with a "life" which cannot die. To "shrink back," as the same seer in the same breath warns us, is to lose the smile of God in a final ruin. But that, for us, cannot be ; we, in His mercy, relying upon the faithful Promiser, attain " the saving of the soul."

Now, as then, the tenth chapter of the Hebrews points with a golden rod to the one path of life, and peace, and perseverance to the end. " Rejoice in the Lord ; *for you it is safe* " (Phil. iii. 1). The " boldness " of a humble assurance of a present and a great salvation traces the way for us, as it traced the way of old, through holiness to Heaven.

8

Faith and Its Power

Hebrews 11

THE eleventh chapter of the Hebrews is a
pre-eminent Scripture. With the fullest
recognition of the Divine greatness of the whole
Bible, never forgetting that "every scripture
hath in it the Spirit of God " (2 Tim. iii. 16),
we are yet aware as we read that some volumes
in the inspired Library are more pregnant than
others, some structures in the sacred city of the
Bible more impressive than others, more rich in
interest, more responsive to repeated visits. Such
a scripture among books is this Epistle, and
such a scripture among chapters is that on
which we enter now.

It is impressive by the majestic singleness of
its theme ; Faith, from first to last, is its matter
and its burthen. Further, it carries one long
appeal to the heart by its method ; almost from
the exordium to the very close it deals with its
theme not by abstract reasoning, nor even by a

citation of inspired utterances only. It works
out its message by a display, in long and living
procession, of inspired human experiences. It
is to an extraordinary degree human, dealing
all along with names as familiar to us as any
in any history can be; with characters which
are perfectly individual; with lives lived in the
face of difficulty, danger, trial, sorrow, as concrete
as possible; with deaths met and overcome under
conditions of mystery, suspense, trial to courage
and to trust, which for all time the heart of man
can apprehend in their solemnity. Meanwhile,
as a matter of diction and eloquence, the chapter
carries in it that peculiar charm which comes
always with a stately enumeration. It has often
been remarked that there is a spell in the mere
recitation of names by a master of verse:

> "Lancelot, and Pelleas, and Pellenore."

Or take that great scene in *Marmion*, where
the spectral summons is pealed from Edinburgh
Cross:

> "Then thunder'd forth a roll of names;
> The first was thine, unhappy James!
> Then all thy nobles came;
> Crawford, Glencairn, Montrose, Argyle,
> Ross, Bothwell, Forbes, Lennox, Lyle,
> Each chief of birth and fame."

And the consummate prose of this our chapter
moves us with the like rhythmical power upon

the spirit, while from Abel and Enoch onwards
we hear recited, name by name, the ancestors of
the undying family of faith. No wonder that
the chapter should have inspired to utterances
formed in its own style the Christian eloquence
of later days, as in that noble closing passage
of Julius Hare's *Victory of Faith,* where he carries
on the record through the apostolic age, and the
early persecutions, and the times of the Fathers,
to Wilfrid and Bernard, the Waldenses, Wiclif,
Luther, Latimer, down to Oberlin, and Simeon,
"and Howard, and Neff, and Henry Martyn."

So we approach the chapter, familiar as it is
(and it is so familiar because it is so great), with
a peculiar and reverent expectation. We look
forward to another visit to this great gallery of
"the portraits of the family of God" with a
pleasure as natural as it is reverent and believing. True to our plan in these expositions,
however, we shall not attempt to comment
upon it in the least degree fully or in detail.
Our aim will be rather to collect and focus
together some main elements of its teaching,
particularly in regard of their applicability to
our own days.

The first question suggested as we read is,
what is the connexion of the chapter? Why
does the Writer spend all this wealth of example
and application upon the one word Faith?

The reason is not far to seek. The tenth
chapter closes with that word, or rather with
that truth: " My righteous man shall live by
faith "; " we are of them that have faith, unto
the saving of the soul." And this close is only
the issue of a strain of previous teachings, going
far back towards the opening of the Epistle.
" The evil heart of unbelief," of " unfaith," if the
word may be used, is the theme of warning in
iii. 12 : " They could not enter in because of
unbelief" (iii. 19). " The word of hearing did
not profit them" because of their lack of faith
(iv. 2). It is " we who have believed" who
" enter into God's rest" (iv. 3). Looking to our
great High Priest and His finished work, we are
to "draw near with a true heart, in fulness of
faith" (x. 22), for the all-sufficient reason that
such trust meets and appropriates eternal truth :
" He is faithful that promised" (x. 23).

These explicit occasional *mentions* of faith are,
however, as we might expect, only a part of the
phenomenon of the great place which *the idea* of
faith holds in the Epistle. When we come to
reflect upon it, the precise position of the Hebrew
Christians was that of men seriously, even tre-
mendously, tempted to walk by sight, not by faith.
The Gospel called them to venture their all, for
time and eternity, upon an invisible Person, an invisible order, a mediation carried on above the

skies, a presentation of sacrifice made in a temple infinitely other than that of Mount Moriah, and a kingdom which, as to all outward appearance, belonged to a future quite isolated from the present. On the other hand, so they were told by their friends, and so it was perfectly natural to them to think, the vast visible institutions of the Law were the very truth of God for their salvation, and those institutions appealed to them through every sense. Why should they forsake a creed which unquestionably connected itself with Divine action and revelation in the past, and which presented itself actually to them under the embodiment of a widespread but coherent nation, all descended from Abraham and Israel, and of a glorious "city of solemnities," and of a temple which was itself a wonder of the world, and of which every detail was "according to a pattern" of Divine purpose, and in which all the worship, all the ritual, done at the altars and within the veil, was great with the majesty of Divine prescription? There the pious Israelite could behold one vast sacramental symbol of JEHOVAH's life, glory, and faithfulness. And the living priesthood that ministered there, in all its courses and orders, was one large, accessible organ of personal witness to the blessings assured to the faithful "child of the Law."

It demands an effort—and it well deserves an
effort—to realize in some measure what the
trial must have been for the sensitive mind of
many a Jewish convert to look thus from the
Gospel to the Law as both shewed themselves to
him then. Even now the earnest and religious
Jew, invited to accept the faith of Jesus, has his
tremendous difficulties of thought, as we well
know, although for so many ages Jerusalem has
been "trodden down," and the priesthood and
sacrifices have become very ancient history.
But when our Epistle was written it was far
otherwise. True, the great ruin of the old order
was very near at hand, but not to the common
eye and mind. It may be—for all things are
possible—that the Papal system may be near
its period; but certainly there is little look of it
to the traveller who visits Rome and contem-
plates St. Peter's and the Vatican. As little did
the end of the Mosaic age present itself as
probable, judging by externals, to the pilgrim to
Jerusalem then, when, for example, the innumer-
able hosts of Passover-keepers filled the whole
environs of the city, and moved incessantly
through the vast courts around the sacred space
where the great altar sent up its smoke morning
and evening, and where the wonderful House
stood intact, "a mountain of snow pinnacled
with gold."

Think of the contrast between such historic invitations to "walk by sight" towards the bosom of Abraham, and the call to "come out and be separate" in some Christian upper-room, devoid of every semblance of decorative art and dignified proportion, only to listen to the Word, to pray and praise in the name of the Crucified, and to eat and drink at the simple Eucharist, the rite of Thanksgiving for — the Master's awful death!

Recollecting these facts of the position, it is no wonder that the Writer emphasizes the greatness and glory of faith, and that now he devotes this whole noble and extended chapter to illustrate that glory.

We come thus to the opening words of the passage, and listen to him as he takes the word "faith" up, and sets it apart, to look afresh at its significance and to describe its potency, before he proceeds, with the tact and skill of sympathy, to illustrate his account of it from the history so deeply sacred to the tried Hebrew Christian's heart.

"Now faith is the assurance of things hoped for, the proving of things not seen." So the Revisers translate the first verse. They place in their margin, as an alternative, a rendering which makes faith to be "the giving substance to things hoped for, the test of things not seen." I presume to think that the margin is preferable as a representation of the first clause in the Greek, and the text as a representation of the second. So I would render (with the one further variation, in view of the Greek, that I dispense with the definite article): "Now faith is a giving of substance to things hoped for, a demonstration of things not seen." And we may paraphrase this rendering somewhat thus: "Faith is that by which the hoped-for becomes to us as if visible and tangible, and by which the unseen is taken and treated as proven in its verity." *

In the light of what we have recalled regarding the position of the first readers of the words, we have only to render them thus to see their perfect appropriateness, their adjustment to an "exceeding need." The Gospel led its disciple supremely and ultimately always towards the hoped-for and the unseen. True, it had a reference of untold value and power to the seen and present. There was then, as there is in

---

* A friend has pointed out to me that in the recently discovered papyri, which, although a relatively small part of them only has been read as yet, have thrown much deeply interesting light on the character and vocabulary of Greek as used by the New Testament writers, the word ὑπόστασις is found with the meaning of "title-deeds." On the hypothesis of such a meaning here (we can only speak with reserve), we may paraphrase: "Faith enables us to treat things hoped for as a property of which we hold the deeds."

our day, nothing like the Gospel to transfigure
character, on the spot, here and now, and thus
to transfigure the scene and the persons around
the man, before his eyes, within reach of his
hands, in the whole intercourse of his life, by
giving them all a new and wonderful yet most
practical importance through the Lord's relation
to them and to him. But it does this always
and inevitably in the power and in the light of
facts which are out of sight now, and of prospects
essentially bound up with "the life of the world
to come." The most diligent and sensible
worker in Christian philanthropy, *if he is fully
Christian* in his idea and action, does what he
does so well for the relief of the oppressed, or
for the civilization of the degraded, because at
the heart of his useful life he spiritually knows
" Him that is invisible," and is animated by the
thought that he works for beings capable, after
this life's discipline, of " enjoying Him fully for
ever." He labours for man, man on earth,
because he loves God in heaven, and because he
believes that God made man and redeemed man
for an immortality to which time is only the short
while all-important avenue. In the calmest
and most normal Christian periods, accordingly,
for the least perilous and heroic forms of faithful
Christian service, it is vital to remember that
attitude and action of the soul which we call

faith. For faith is essential both to the victories and the utilities of the Christian life, just so far as that life touches always at its living spring "things hoped for," "things not seen." And at a time like that of the first readers of the Epistle every such necessity was enhanced indefinitely, both by the perils and threatenings which they had to face and by the majestic illusion to which they were continually exposed—the illusion under which the order of the Law, because it was Divine in origin and magnificent in its visible embodiment, looked as if it must be the permanent, the final, phase of sacred truth and life on earth.

In our next chapter we will consider both the account of faith here given and some main points in the illustration of it by examples.

9

Faith and Its Annals

Hebrews 11

WE considered in the last chapter the account
of Faith with which the apostolic Writer
opens this great recital of the " life, work, and
triumph of faith" in holy human lives. His words,
as we found, lend themselves to some variety of
explanation in detail : the term ὑπόστασις alone
may be interpreted in at least three ways. But
I do not think that this need disturb us as to
the essential meaning of the description. Each
and all of the renderings leave us with the thought
that faith has a power in it to make the thing
hoped-for act upon us as if it were attained, and
the invisible as if it were before our eyes.

We may pause so far further over the
description of faith here as to point out that it
is precisely this, a description, not a definition.
To quote Heb. xi. 1 as a good definition of faith
is to mistake its import altogether. I have
often recalled, in speech or writing, a story told

me forty years ago by an Oxford friend when we were masters together at a public school. He had attended a Greek Testament lecture at his college a few years before, and the lecturer one day asked the class for a definition of faith. Some one quoted Heb. xi. 1, and the lecturer's answer was, "You could not have given a worse definition." My old friend, a "broad" but most reverent Churchman, referred to this as an instance of painful flippancy. It may have been so. But I am prepared to think that the lecturer may not have meant it so at all. He may only have expressed rather crudely his view, the right view, to my mind, that we have here not a definition of faith at all but a description of faith as an operative force, an account of what faith looks like when it is at work; and this is a very different matter.

What is a definition? A precise and exclusive statement of the essentials of a thing, such that it will fit no other thing. A description may be something altogether different from this. It may so handle the object that the terms are not exclusive at all, but are equally applicable to something else; as here for example, where the phraseology would equally well describe imagination in its more vivid forms—a thing as different as possible from faith. To be quite practical, we have here, if we read this first verse in the light of the whole subsequent development of the chapter, a description of faith at work, of the potency and victories of faith, rather than a definition of faith in its distinctive essence. A true parallel to this passage is the familiar sentence, " Knowledge is power." Those words do not define knowledge, obviously ; to do that would demand a totally different phrase. What the words do is to give us one great resultant of knowledge ; to tell us that the possession and use of knowledge endows the man who knows with a force and efficiency which he would lack without it. Few words are more elastic and adaptable than the verb substantive. " *Is* " can denote a wide variety of ideas, from that of personal identity, as when I see that yonder distant figure *is* my brother ; to that of equivalence, as when a stamped and signed piece of thin paper called a bank-note *is* five pounds of gold ; or to that of mere representation, as when another piece of paper, or a sheet of canvas, duly lined and coloured by the artist to show the semblance of a human face, *is* the King, or *is* my father ; or to that of result and effect, as when we say that knowledge *is* power, or that seeing *is* believing.*

---

* It is obvious that these elementary reflections have everything to do with the need of caution in explaining those most sacred words, ''This *is* my body which is given for you.''

Here we have precisely that last application of the verb substantive, only in an exact and most noble antithesis. " Seeing is believing," says the familiar proverb. " Believing is seeing," says the Divine word here. That is to say, when the human soul so relies upon God that His word is absolute and sufficient for its certainties, this reliance, this faith, has in it the potency of sight. It is as sure of the promised blessing as if it were a present possession. It is as ready to act upon " the things not seen as yet," the laws, powers, hopes beyond the veil, as if all was in open view to the eyes of the body.

The whole course of the chapter, when it comes down to particulars and persons, bears this out. From first to last the message carried to us by the lives and actions of the faithful is this, that they took their Lord at His word, simply as His word, and in the power of that reliance found themselves able to act as if the unseen were seen and the hoped-for were present. " The elders " (ver. 2) are in view from the first —that is to say, the pre-Christian saints, who were in *that* sense distinctively men who proved the power of faith, that they all lived and died before the visible fulfilment of the great promise of salvation. To them, to be sure, or rather to many of them, not to all, merciful helps were granted. The unseen and the hoped-for was sometimes, not always, made more tangible to them by the grant of some sign and token, some portent or miracle, by the way. But the careful Bible-reader knows how very little such things are represented in the holy histories as being the " daily bread " of the life of the old believers. Even in the lives where they occur most often they come at long and difficult intervals, and in some lives not at all, or hardly at all. And assuredly we gather here that, to the mind of the apostolic Writer, no experience of miracles, no permission even to hold direct colloquy with the Eternal, ever made up for that immeasurable " aid to faith " which we enjoy who know the Incarnate Son as fact, and walk on an earth which has seen the God-Man traverse it, and die upon it, and rise again.

These " elders " were men called to live, in an eminent and most trying degree, not by sight but by faith, by mere reliance upon a Promiser. Therefore their living witness to the capacity of faith to make the unseen visible and the hoped-for present is the more precious to us. We, with the Christ of God manifested to us, displayed in history, experienced in the heart—what are not we to find the power of faith to be in our lives, having, for our supreme seal upon faith, the promise fulfilled, the Image

of the Invisible God, made one with our nature
and dwelling in our hearts ?

One partial exception, and only one, to this
great ruling lesson of the chapter is to be
noted; it occurs in the second verse. There
" by faith we perceive that the worlds," the
æons, the dispensations and evolutions of created
being, " have been framed," perfected, adjusted
to one another, " by the Word of God, so that
not from things which appear has that which
is seen originated." These words appear to be
inserted where they stand in order, so to speak,
to carry the sequence of the references to the
Old Testament down from its very first page.
The work of faith has exercise in face of the
mysterious narrative of Creation, and in this
one instance the exercise is quoted as what
concerns us now quite as much as " the elders."
They like us, we like them, get our guarantee
as to the facts of the primal past not by sight
but by faith, by taking God at His word. He,
in His revelation, tells us that " in the beginning "—the beginning of whatever existence
is other than eternal—" God created." Things
finite, things visible, came into original being
not as evolved from previous similar material,
but as of His will.

But when that pregnant side-word has once
been said, the argument settles itself forthwith

upon the recorded examples of the potency of
faith as " the elders " exercised it. We see man
after man enabled to treat the invisible as visible,
the promised as present, by reliant rest upon the
word of God, however conveyed. To Abel, we
know not how, it was divinely said that the
sacrificed " firstling " was the acceptable offering,
and, antecedent to any possible experience, he
offered it. To Enoch, we know not how, it
was made known that the Eternal, as invisible
to him as to us, cared for man's worshipping
company, and he addressed himself through his
age-long life to " walk with God." Noah was
apprised, for the first time in man's known
history, of an approaching cataclysm and of the
way of escape ; the promise came to him wrapped
in the cloud of an awful warning, and it was
long delayed, but he acted upon it in the steady
energy of faith. Abraham was " called," we know
not precisely how, but in some way which tested
his reliance on things " not seen as yet," and he
set out on that wonderful life of a hundred
years of faith. He renounced the settled habits
and old civilization of Chaldea for the new life
of a Syrian nomad, " settling permanently in
tents " (ἐν σκηναῖς κατοικήσας), he and his son
and his grandson after him, all in view of an
invisible future made visible by the trusted
promise, a future culminating at last to his " eye

of faith," so here we are solemnly assured, in
the city of the saints, in the Canaan of the
heavens. The same reliance on the sheer word
of promise nerved him to the awful ordeal of the
all-but immolation of his son. And that son
in his turn, against all appearances, and rather
bowing to the Word of God than embracing it,
blessed *his* least-loved son above his dearest;
and that son in his turn, and his son in his turn,
carried the process on, treating the greatness of
Ephraim and the deliverance from Egypt as
things seen and present, because God had so
spoken. The parents of Moses, and then Moses
himself, in his strange life of disappointments
and wonders, deal likewise with the future, the
unseen, the seemingly impossible, on the warrant
of a promise. Figures as little heroic in natural
character as Sarah, as little noble in life as
Rahab, take place in the long procession, as
those who treat the invisible as visible by faith.
So do the thronging "elders" of ver. 32—a
group singularly diverse in everything but this
victory over the seen and present by faith in
the promise. So do the unnamed confessors and
martyrs of the closing paragraph, the heart-
broken, the tortured, the wanderers of the dens
and caves, who all alike, amidst a thousand
differences of condition and of character, "obtained a good report through faith"; and all

won through faith that victory, so great when we reflect upon it—that they died "not having received the promise." They trusted *to the very end.* When they sank down in death upon their shadowy path of pilgrimage, "the promise," the promised Christ, had not yet come. Nevertheless they treated the hope of Him as fact, and they won their victory by faith.

And now they are parts and members of the "great cloud" who watch us in our turn—us, with things unseen and hoped-for still in front, but with JESUS at our side.

10

Followers of Them

Hebrews 12: 1-14

THE Epistle approaches its close. The Writer
has much yet to say to the disciples upon
many things, all connected with that main
interest of their lives, a resolute fidelity to the
Lord, to the Gospel, and to one another. But
he has not yet quite done with that side of their
"exceeding need" to which the antidote is *the
faith* which can deal with the future as the
present, with the unseen as the seen. Upon
this theme, from one aspect or another, is spent
the passage now before us.

First, the appeal is to the recollection that
the combat, the race, the victory of faith, as it
was for the Hebrew believers, "the contest set
before *us*" (ver. 1), not only had been fought
and won before them by the saints of the old
time, but that those saints were now, from
their blessed rest, as "spirits of the just made
perfect" (ver. 23), watchers and witnesses of

their successors' course. "We have, lying around us, so great a cloud of witnesses" (ver. 1). "We" are running, like the competitors in the Hellenic stadium, in the public view of a mighty concourse, so vast, so aggregated, so placed aloft, that no word less great than "cloud" occurs as its designation: that "long cloud" as it is finely called in Isaac Watts' noble hymn, "Give me the wings of faith." True, the multitudinous watchers are unseen, but this only gives faith another opportunity of exercise; we are to treat the Blessed as seen, for we know that they are there, living to God, one with us, fellows of our life and love. So let us address ourselves afresh to the spiritual race, the course of faith. Let us, as athletes of the soul, strip all encumbrance off, "every weight" of allowed wrong, all guilty links with the world of rebellion and self-love; "the sin which doth so easily beset us," clinging so soon around the feet, like a net of fine but stubborn meshes, till the runner gives up the hopeless effort and is lost.*

I thus explain the "witnesses" to mean spectators, watchers, not testifiers. The con-

---

* I cannot think possible the alternative (marginal) rendering of εὐπερίστατον in the Revised Version — "*admired by many.*" There is example for the meaning in classical Greek, but *the idea* is totally out of keeping with the spirit of this passage.

text seems to me to decide somewhat positively
for this explanation. It is an altogether
pictorial context; the imagery of the foot-race
comes suddenly up, and in a moment raises
before us the vision of the stadium and its
surroundings. The reader cannot see the course
with his inner eyes without also seeing those
hosts of eager lookers-on which made, on every
such occasion, in the old world as now, the life
of the hour. In such a context nothing but
explicit and positive reasons to the contrary
could give to the word "witnesses," and to the
word "cloud" in connexion with it, any other
allusion. True, these watchers are all, as a fact,
evidential "witnesses" also, testifiers to the
infinite benefit and success of the race of faith.
But that thought lies almost hidden behind the
other. It is as loving, sympathetic, inspiring
lookers-on that the old saints, from Abel onwards, are here seen gathered, thronging and
intent, around us as we run.

The conception runs off of course into
mystery, as every possible conception about the
unseen does, even when Scripture is most
explicit about unseen facts. We ask, and ask
in vain, what is the medium through which
these observers watch us, the air and light, as it
were, in which their vision acts; what is their
proximity to us all the while; to what extent

they are able to know the entire conditions of
our race. But all this leaves faith in peaceful
possession of a fact of unspeakable animation.
It tells the discouraged or tired Christian,
tempted to think of the unseen as a dark
void, that it is rather a bright and populous
world, in mysterious touch and continuity with
this, and that our forerunners, from those
of the remotest past down to the last-called
beloved one who has passed out of our
sight, know enough about us to mark our
advance and to prepare their welcome at the
goal.

In that rich treasury of sacred song, *Hymns
from the Land of Luther*, is included the translation of a noble hymn by Simon Dach, *O wie
selig seid ihr doch, ihr Frommen*, "O how happy
are ye, saints forgiven." That hymn beautifully
illustrates this verse. It is written responsively
all through. One stanza, sung upward, is the
utterance from below of the pilgrim Church,
longing for her rest. The next, sung from
above, is the answer of the Blessed, telling of
their love and sympathy, taught them by their
own similar sufferings, of their bright foreview
of the celestial crown reserved for their still
toiling brethren. So the two choirs answer each
other, turn by turn, till at last both join in a
glorious concert of blended song, a closing strain

of faith and praise. Let us listen often for
those answers from above.

But the holy Writer has more to say yet
about the motives to faith. He points the
weary saints upward, even beyond the "cloud,"
to a Form radiant and supreme. They are to
run, conscious of the witnesses, but yet more
intently "looking off (ἀφορῶντες) unto JESUS,
the supreme Leader (ἀρχηγόν) and Perfecter of
faith"; that is to say, the Lord of the whole
host of the believing, and Himself the consummate Worker in the field of faith, who, for a
joy promised *but not seen*, "endured the Cross,"
when its immediate aspect was an inexpressible
outrage and disgrace; reaching the throne of
all existence, as Son of Man, in spite of every
possible appearance to the contrary (ver. 2).
Yes, and not only was that final victory thus won
by Him, but He arrived at it by a path full of
the conflicts which threaten faith. He "endured
the contradiction of sinners against Himself"
(ver. 3). Year by year, day by day, from the
Pharisee, from the worldling, from the leaders
of religion, from the inconstant crowd, He had
"contradiction" to endure—sometimes even from
"the men of His own household." He was
challenged to prove His claims; He was insulted
over His assertion of them, or over His silence
about them. In every way, at every turn, they

spoke against Him to His face, as He slowly
advanced, through a life of love and suffering, to
the Agony and the Crucifixion.

Let us not think that all this put no strain,
even in the King Messiah, upon faith. It may
seem scarcely reverent (I know devout and
thoughtful Christians who have felt it to be
so) to speak of our blessed Lord as exercising
faith, as being the supreme Believer. But we
need not shrink from the thought. It is no more
irreverent, surely, than to accept the evidence
of the Gospels to His perfect human capacity
to be weary, to be surprised, to be specially
moved to compassion by *the sight* of suffering.
In His sinless conformity "in all things to His
brethren" there was never for one moment
room in Him—of this we may be amply sure
—for error of thought or of word, as He acted
as the supreme and absolute Prophet of His
Church. But there was room, so we are expressly told, on one tremendous occasion at
least (Matt. xxvi. 37), for a mysterious "be-
wilderment" (ἀδημονεῖν) of His blessed human
soul. Can we doubt that the victory won in
the Garden, after which He went with profound
calmness to the unjust priest, and Pilate, and
the Cross, was of the nature of a victory of
faith? Did He not then treat the coming "joy"
as a reality although, in so awful a sense and

measure. He did not "feel" it then? The "be-
wilderment" did not drive Him back from our
redemption; and why? Because "He TRUSTED
in GOD that He would deliver Him" (Ps. xxii. 9 ;
Matt. xxvii. 42), whatever should be the contents of "the cup" from which His whole
humanity turned away as *almost* impossible to
drink.

And may we not be sure that on many a
previous occasion of minor and yet bitter trial,
when evil men gathered round Him with cynical
objections and ruthless denials of His claims,
the victory was akin to the victory of Geth-
semane? Often, surely, a strange "bewilder-
ment" must have beset the Redeemer's soul, of
which the external token was the sigh, the
groan, the tears, which shewed Him to be so
truly Man.

We all hold, in full doctrinal orthodoxy, that
the Lord's sufferings, both of soul and body, were
no "docetic" semblance but a deep and infinitely
pathetic reality. But we need at times to think
somewhat deliberately in order to receive the
full impression of that truth upon the heart.
And then surely we are constrained to see in
Him, who thus really suffered and really "endured," the supreme Exemplar of the victory
of faith, the perfect Sympathizer with the tried
believer.

From this pregnant thought, of the faith exercised by JESUS, the disciple is directly led in the remainder of our passage to the practical inferences for himself. The days, for those first readers of the Epistle, were indeed evil. Though not yet called to martyrdom (ver. 4), they were hard beset, not only by importunate reasonings and appeals which, as we have seen all along, were straining their spiritual allegiance, but by actual outrages (see *e.g.* x. 34), by the "scourging" (ver. 6) of bitter social persecution. Well, "looking off unto" Him who had so greatly endured, they were, in these things also, to see the unseen and to presentiate the future. From the Proverbs (iii. 11, 12), that book where the apostolic insight so often finds the purest spiritual messages,* he quotes (verses 5, 6) the tender words which bid the chastened child see in his chastening the assurance (ver. 8) of his happy, holy sonship in the home of a Father, "the Father of our spirits," who, unlike our earthly fathers even at their best (and that was a noble best indeed), not only chastens, but chastens with an unerring result of holiness in the submissive child—yea, a holiness which is one with His own (ver. 10), His Spirit in our wills.

* It was evidently a book dear to St. Peter's mind, as his First Epistle shews.

Beautiful is *the sympathy* of this appeal to live, by faith, the life of victorious patience. "All chastening, for the present, seems not to belong to joy but grief" (ver. 11). Yes, the immediate pain is here fully recognized, not ignored. It is not spoken of as if, in view of its sequel, it did not matter. "It belongs to grief." Scripture is full of this tender insight into the bitterness of even our salutary sorrows, and its appeals to patience are all the more potent for that insight. "Nevertheless, afterward, it produces the peace-bringing fruit of righteousness," the sense of a profound inward rest, found in conformity to the "sweet, beloved will of God," in living correspondence to the Father's rule, "for those who have been exercised, as in a spiritual *gymnasium* (γεγυμνασμένοις), thereby." That "exercise" was to tell at once, as they surrendered their wills to it in faith, in a present sense of the certainty of future blessing. "Brace the slack hands" to toil, "and the unstrung knees" to march (ver. 12), "and make straight paths for your feet," using your will, faith-strengthened, to choose the line of the will of God, and that alone. So should "the lame thing" be "healed" rather than "turned aside." The walk, feeble and halting always when the will is divided, should be restored to firmness and certainty again.

"Nevertheless, afterward." That is the watchword of the whole pregnant passage. Nature, shortsighted and impatient, can deal with the seen and the present only. Grace, in its victorious form of patient faith, already takes hold upon the "afterward," and works on, and walks on, "as seeing Him that is invisible."

With the thought of the witness-cloud around us, and "looking off" to the Prince of Faith, ascended, yet present with us, and sure of the ultimate and eternal "fruit of righteousness" which lies hidden in the chastening of the Father of our spirits—we too will live by faith, taking God at His word, and saying Amen to His will, even to the end.

11

Sinai and Sion

Hebrews 12: 14-28

THE paragraph before us is largely concerned with the inner life of the believing community, its cohesion member with member, and the call to each member and to all to "walk warily in dangerous days," in the path of evangelical holiness. The Writer lays it upon them (ver. 14) to "pursue peace with all," such peace as always *tends*, even in bad times, to reward the "sons of peace," while they so behave themselves as never on their own part to contribute a factor to avoidable strife, and while the influence of their meek consistency leavens in some measure the mass around them. With equal and concurrent care they are to "pursue sanctification." It is to be their strong ambition to develope and deepen incessantly that dedication of themselves to the Holy One which will give them at once the standard and the secret of holiness, by bringing them into immediate

contact with Him who is at once their law and
their life. They are to " live out," in the spirit
of a resolute quest after fuller and yet fuller
attainment, the fact that He has redeemed them
to be "a people of His own possession"; remembering, with a solemn simplicity of conviction, that only "the pure in heart" shall
ever be able to "see God." For the spirit
which refuses to come into a surrendered
harmony with His Spirit might be set in the
midst of heaven itself, yet it would be blind, it
would be blinded—by that *alien* glory. They are
to keep watch and oversight upon one another
(ver. 15), mutually observant all round, to see
that the life of faith and love is alive indeed.
Does any one find his fellow-believer "falling
short of the grace of God," sinking into conduct
no better than the world's ? This must at once
disquiet the observer, and call out his loving
warnings, or at least his anxious intercessions ;
for the declining convert inevitably extends an
influence of decline around him, and the issue
will be, in the end, a declining Church. Is "any
root of bitterness growing up"? Is there (see
Deut. xxix. 18) any Christian in the company
so fallen, so "embittered" by alienation from his
Lord, as to be a cause around him of "defile-
ment," so as to stain ultimately large circles
(οἱ πολλοί) with the deep pollution of a practical

apostasy from holiness? Is there here and there
a personal example of spiritual infidelity (πόρνος)
to the Lord, of that radically " secular " (βέβηλος)
spirit (ver. 16) of which Esau is the type, to
which some " mess of meat," some material ad-
vantage, proves overwhelmingly more momentous
than the unworldly " birthright " given by the
promise of God? Let them all watch as for
their life against such symptoms. It is a matter
of eternal import. The ancient Esau found too
late that he was an outcast, irrevocably, from the
great blessing, though then he cried for it with
a cry great and bitter. In vain he asked his
father to reverse the destiny; there was no
" place of repentance " in Isaac's will, for Isaac
knew that he had but carried out, blind as he
was, the will of God.

Then follows (verses 18–24) that sublime
antithesis of Sinai and Sion which forms one of
the greatest examples of rhythmical, of almost
lyrical, eloquence in the whole New Testament.
On the one hand looms on the view the Thing,*
material, tangible (ψηλαφωμένῳ), all on fire,
black with tempestuous cloud, its echoes pealing
(ver. 19) to a tremendous trumpet-blast and then
to a yet more awful " voice of words." At its

* The word ὄρει is certainly absent from the true text. We
are left as in presence of a mysterious *somewhat*, a mighty mass,
mantled in terror and without form or name.

base cowers an awe-struck, horror-struck, host of men, shuddering at the warning (ver. 20) not to touch the fatal rocks, crowding for refuge round a leader who himself owns (ver. 21) to heart-shaking fears.* On the other hand, as the eyes of faith are lifted, there shines into view, and in the closest spiritual proximity (for the believing company has actually "come unto it," ver. 22), the hill eternal, the true Mount Sion, where shines the city of the living God, the Jerusalem of heaven. No barren rocks are there, nor do menaces of articulate thunder sound from and around that height. All is light, and all is life. Yes, above all things all is life. Behold the countless thousands (μυριάσιν) of radiant denizens, the angelic friends of man; and then beatified men besides (ver. 23), "festal assembly and church of the first-born, enrolled in heaven"; the Blessed gone before, the "great cloud," seen now in their other character, as the triumphant throng of a celestial Passover, or of a Tabernacle-feast of palms, kept in the better Canaan to commemorate the mercies of the mortal wilderness. And there, centre and sun of the wonderful scene, is the glory of the "Judge of all," Vindicator (so we read the meaning of the word κριτής here) of His afflicted ones, treading

---

* A traditional utterance must be referred to. But the whole narrative in Exodus and in Deuteronomy supports it.

down their enemies and presiding in majesty
over their happy estate. Around Him rest and
rejoice the pure "spirits of the just made
perfect," the dear and holy who have lately
passed through death, "perfected" already, even
before their resurrection, in respect of the course
finished, the fight fought, the faith kept, the
trial for ever over. Lastly (ver. 24), the form
is seen of the more than Moses of this better
Mount of God. Behold the Mediator, not of the
old covenant but of the new, the Covenant of
the Eternal Spirit. Behold the Surety of the
promise of the purified heart, the promise sealed
with that sprinkled blood of the Incarnate
Lamb which, in Divine antithesis to the call
for vengeance on the fratricide which went up
from Abel's death, claims for the "brethren" who
once slew their Deliverer not remission only but
holiness and heaven.

It is a wonderful picture, the hill of the awful
Law confronted by the "hill whence cometh our
help." And we ask ourselves why, just here in
the Epistle, it is painted for us and left upon
our spirit's eyes for ever. Surely it is that the
Hebrew disciple (and we in our turn to-day)
may be quickened in watching and in walk-
ing alike by an immense encouragement and a
warning of corresponding power. The call has
just been made, all through the twelfth chapter

up to this point, to endure, to watch, to warn each other, to pursue to the uttermost the ambition of holiness. Let this be done as by those whose pilgrim tents are pitched as it were in a valley between those two mountains of God. Let the true Israelite turn his eyes sometimes upon Sinai, to learn again from its shadows and its thunders the infinite importance of the eternal Will, the awfulness of transgression, the terrors of the Law when its demand is met only by the miserable failures of the sinner. Then, humbled lower than the dust, let him turn towards the eternal Sion, and not only turn towards it but recollect that in the Spirit, and in the Son, he has "*come unto it.*" In the Lord Christ, his better Moses, his saving Mediator, he has already arrived beside it and rests upon it. No voice of thunder bids him not to touch it "lest he be thrust through." He is commanded to come as near to it as it is possible to be, because he is to come to "the Lord of the Hill" Himself, in the absolute proximity of faith, love, and life. He is welcomed to its recesses, and to its heights. The first-born are his brethren; the just made perfect are his own beloved; every angel of all the host is his friend; the supreme Judge is his omnipotent Protector; Jesus is his Peace, through the blood of His Cross. "Blest inhabitant of Sion, washed in the Redeemer's blood!" Shall he

not address himself to the path and pursuit
of holiness with a heart beating with an inex-
haustible hope, and with a life present while
eternal ?

Then, as the great paragraph approaches its
climax, the note of warning sounds again
(ver. 25). The convert, fresh from the reminder
of the "voice" of the sprinkled blood of the
better covenant, is cautioned not to "refuse" it,
not to "decline" it (μὴ παραιτήσησθε). The
primary reference is manifestly to that perpetual
danger of the Hebrews, the temptation to turn
back from the Gospel, with its spiritual order and
its hopes of things not yet seen, to the outworn
Dispensation, with its externally majestic circumstances of glorious ritual and imposing shows of
polity and power. They would need again and
again to open the soul's ears and eyes, and steadfastly to recollect, against all appearances, that we
"*are come unto* the Mount Sion," if they were to
resist the magnetic forces which drew them back
towards Sinai—and towards death. So they were
to hear the sweet voices of heavenly love, and
festal life, and blood-bought covenanted peace,
sounding from the true Sion, with joy indeed but
also with holy dread. They were to *fear* lest
they should "decline" them, lest sense should
conquer faith and the soul be lost under the
mountain of condemnation after all. "For if

they did not escape who on earth declined Him who spoke oraculous warning (χρηματίζοντα), much more shall we not escape, turning from Him who warns from heaven" (ver. 25). The contemner of the ban of Sinai fell "stricken through" the body. The "decliner" of the admonition to turn no more to the hill of doom, but boldly to climb the hill of peace, will fall stricken through the soul. That warning voice, which once shook the desert, has now promised (ver. 26)—for a promise, the promise of an eternal redemption, lies deep in that threatening (Hag. ii. 6)—that not earth only but heaven is yet to feel His shaking, and once for ever when it comes. He, "yet once more," shall work one vast "removing"; and then (ver. 27) a stability irremovable shall finally come in. "The things that have been made," the terrestrial and material "figures of the real" (ix. 24), are to pass away, never to return, in order that "the things incapable of disturbance" (τὰ μὴ σαλευό-μενα) "may remain." And what are these things? Nothing less than the spiritual, ulti-mate, all-fulfilling truths and glories to which the "things made" served as preparation, type, and foil, but which themselves to all eternity shall know no successors, no "new order" through which God shall otherwise "fulfil Himself." For what are they, in their inmost essence? They

are the truths which spring always from the
Incarnate Son, and return always into Him;
"the redemption that is in Christ Jesus, with
eternal glory."

So let the disciples clasp their sublime
privileges, and greatly rejoice — and also
greatly fear to "decline" them, to surrender
them, to treat them lightly. They "are in
receipt (παραλαμβάνοντες) of a kingdom un-
shakable," for they have become the willing
vassals of the eternal David of the true Israel, in
whose kingship they too are kings, reigning over
"all the power of the enemy." But, for the
very reason that they hold a royalty, and such a
royalty, let them address themselves to a life of
adoration, and reverence, and awe, deep as that
of the holy ones who, close to the throne above,
veil their faces and their feet evermore with
their wings, not in terror but in a joy full of
wonder and of worship. "Let us have grace,"
let us *take and use* the grace which in the
covenant is ours,* and in it let us live this life.
For it is to be a life all the while not of alarm
and doubting, but *of grace.* Only it is to be
lived as before Him who is (ver. 29) "consuming
fire, a jealous God" (Deut. iv. 24), "jealous"
against all "forsakers of their own mercy"

* For this use of ἔχωμεν compare Rom. v. 1, where the best
supported reading gives ἔχωμεν εἰρήνην.

(Jonah ii. 8), rejectors of His Son, even when they seem to fly for refuge to His Law.

Thus the great concatenated passage concludes with one of the most formidable of Scripture utterances. But let us boldly gather peace and hope even from this word of fire. For what is the true message of the verses we have traversed, when we look back and sum them up? It is the glory, the fulness, the living richness, the abundant lovingkindness, the supreme and absolute finality, of the Gospel of our Lord Jesus Christ. It is our Lord Himself, the perfect and ultimate revelation of the grace and peace of God. And the fiery jealousy of the close, the warning that we shall lose our souls if we " decline " the blessed Son, what does it mean as to His Father's heart? That He so loves the Son, and so loves us, that He adjures us by all His terrors as well as all His mercies never to turn for refuge for one hour away from the all-perfect Christ.

12

Appeals and Instructions

Hebrews 13: 1-14

THE last chapter of the Epistle has a character quite of its own. Unlike many of those often arbitrary divisions of the New Testament books which we know as chapters, it is a naturally separate section. The long and sustained arguments are over. The Writer's thoughts, gravitating to a close, and occupied naturally as they do so with the personal conditions of his Hebrew brethren, attach themselves now to one now to another side of their duties, their difficulties, their more particular and detailed needs, practical and spiritual. As he touches upon these, sentence by sentence, we often see at a glance the probable occasion of the words, but often again we are left in the dark about it. Who shall say precisely why he insists (ver. 2) upon the exercise of hospitality ? or who were " the prisoners " (ver. 3) whom he bids them remember ? Who shall tell what in this particular community was the occasion for a solemn emphasis (ver. 4) upon the holiness of marriage, or why again, just for them, it was well to speak in warning (ver. 5) about the love of money and the temptation to discontent? Nor can we be certain who were those departed " leaders," " guides," of ver. 7, whose " faith " the disciples were to " imitate," whose blessed " exit from their walk of life " they were to " contemplate."

All we can say of these opening topics of the chapter is that, whatever the occasions were, the words occasioned are for us inestimably precious. Dear to the heart of the believing Church for ages have been these precepts to love the brethren (φιλαδελφία), to love the stranger (φιλοξενία), to remember Abraham at Mamre and Gideon at Ophrah with their angel-guests, and to see a possible angel-visitor in every needing stranger at the door. The call (ver. 2) to remember the captive, and the sufferer of every sort, comes with solemn power from this paragraph, as it presses home the law of sympathetic fellowship, and in one passing phrase (" *as being in the body* ") reminds us that, for the Christian, all sufferings, all burthens of pain and care, cease for ever when once he is " out of the body." Sacred is the witness borne here to the pure dignity of wedlock (ver. 4):

" Be * marriage honourable in all things, and the
bed unspotted ; for fornicators and adulterers "—
not only adulterers, but those also who sin that
other sin which the world so easily and so
blindly condones—" God will judge." And when
the Christian is warned (ver. 5) against the
greed of gain, the quoted words of the Old
Testament make, by the use they are put to, a
possession for ever valuable to the believing reader
of the Scriptures. For not only are they in
themselves wonderful in their emphasis : " I will
never give thee up ; I will never, never desert
thee." They are inestimable as an example of
the sort of use which this New Testament prophet could make of the spiritual riches of the
Old Testament. For here he sees a Divine
watchword for the new life, not only in the
glorious outburst of faith (ver. 6) in Psalm cxviii.,
the *Hallel* of the Passover. In the words
spoken to Joshua, and to all appearance spoken
to him personally and alone (ver. 5 : see Josh.
i. 5), we are led equally to see a message from
the heart of God straight to every Christian soul.
Seldom, if ever, are we more powerfully and
tenderly encouraged than we are here to use
with confidence that old-fashioned and now often

---

* The sentence demands an understood *imperative* verb, without which the "*for*" which (in the true reading) introduces
the second clause is out of place.

disparaged sort of Bible study, the collection
of eternal and universal principles of spiritual
life out of an "isolated text."

Then comes the passage where the departed
"guides" are commemorated. Whoever they
were, were they a Stephen and a James, or
saints utterly unknown to us, that passage is
precious in its principles, true for all time, of
remembrance and appeal. It consecrates the
fidelity of the Christian memory. It assures us
that to cherish the names, the words, the conduct, the holy lives, the blessed deaths, of our
teachers of days long done is no mere indulgence
of unfruitful sentiment. It is natural to the
Gospel, which, just because it is the message
of an unspeakably happy future, also sanctifies
the past which is the living antecedent to it.
Just because we look with the love of hope towards
"our gathering together unto Him," we are to
turn with the love of memory towards all the
gifts of God given to us through the holy ones
with whom we look to be "gathered together."
"The exit of their walk of life" (ver. 7) is to
be our study, our meditation. We are to "look
it up and down" ($\dot{a}\nu a\theta\epsilon\omega\rho o\hat{v}\nu\tau\epsilon s$) as we would
some great monument of victory, and from that
contemplation we are to go back into life, to
"imitate their faith," to do just what they did,
treating (xi. 1) the unseen as visible, the hoped-

for as present and within our embrace. Thank
God for this authorization and hallowing of our
recollections. Precious indeed is its assurance that
the sweetness of them (for all its ineffable element
of sadness, as eyes and ears are hungry for the
faces and the voices gone, for the look and tone
of the preacher, the teacher, through whom we
first knew the Lord, or knew Him better) is no
half-forbidden luxury of the soul but a means
of victorious grace.

But now comes in a passage of the chapter
which more obviously tells its own story of
occasion and aim. The Writer recurs to the
supreme theme of the Epistle, the antithesis
between the Lord Jesus, with His finished work
and absolute permanence, and the transitory
antecedents of the older dispensation. Once
more the Hebrews are to remember His eternity,
His eternal personal identity, unbeginning and
without end (ver. 8); He is "the same, yester-
day, and to-day, and unto the ages." Before
all types and preparations, before law, and ritual,
and prophecy, He is. When, having done their
long work, they cease, He still is. Over the
glory of His being and character passes no
"shadow of turning." Never to the endless
ages shall He need to be other than He is,
or to be succeeded by a greater. "JESUS,
MESSIAH"; He is Alpha; He is also Omega.

The whole alphabet of revelation between the first letter and the last does but spell out the golden legend of His unalterable glory.

In contrast to Him, thus unchangeably Himself, place the " teachings variegated and alien " (ver. 9) which would draw you from beside Him (παραφέρεσθε) back to an outworn ceremonial distorted from its true purpose. " Looking unto Jesus," stay still and be at rest in Him. The ritual law of "food" (βρώματα) had its perfectly befitting place in the age of elementary preparation. But to make it now a rival to the message of that "grace" which means a life lived by faith in the Son of God, is to defraud " the heart " of that which alone can "establish" it in peace, holiness, and hope. To walk in Him is to go from strength to strength. To "walk in them " (οἱ περιπατοῦντες) is to miss the very "benefit" you seek. It is to move away from the light, backward, into spiritual death.

Here follows in close sequence a passage of pregnant significance. It begins with ver. 10, and the connexion is not finally broken till ver. 16. The Writer, prompted perhaps by the allusion to a ceremonial law of "meats," turns abruptly to the still existing ritual of the Law, familiar to his Hebrew readers as to himself. From it he leads their thoughts once more to the profound import and ultimate efficacy of the supreme atoning Sacrifice, in all its shame and all its glory, and to the call which that great fact conveys to the believer to break for ever, at whatever cost, from the old order, *considered as a rival to the Cross.* Such is the true bearing of this often debated passage, if I am not greatly mistaken. The "altar" which "we have" (ver. 10) is not, if I read the argumentative context rightly, either the atoning Cross, at least as to any direct reference of the word, or the Table of the Christian Eucharist. As to this latter conjecture indeed the reference is totally unsupported by any really primeval parallel.* And *in this Epistle* it is scarcely conceivable that, if that were the meaning, if we were to be abruptly informed here that we Christians have in the Holy Table a sacrificial altar, no allusion, however slight, should intimate that the Christian minister is not a "leader" only but a sacrificing priest. The whole Epistle may be said to circle round the great topic of Priesthood. From various points of view, and with purposes as practical as possible in regard of faith, hope, and life, that topic has been handled. But is it too

---

* Lightfoot (on Ign. *ad Eph.* v., *et alibi*) has clearly shewn that Ignatius' use of θυσιαστήριον is altogether mystical. He means not the Holy Table but (among other references) the Church of Christ as the sphere or place of spiritual sacrifice.

much to say that, for the Writer, the one
Christian priesthood which is analogous to the
Levitical priesthood, as a sacrificial and mediatorial function on behalf of the Church, is the
High Priesthood of the Son of God? The
Christian Ministry indeed hardly, if at all,
comes into view throughout the argument. We
find it at length in this chapter, the chapter
which tells the readers that they "have an
altar." Twice over the pastors of the Church
are mentioned here (verses 7, 17); but how?
As "leaders," "guides," ἡγούμενοι: as those
who "speak the word of God," as those whose
vigilance over the souls of the flock claims a
loving and grateful loyalty. That is to say,
the Christian Ministry is above all things a
pastorate. To a sacerdotal aspect of its special
functions no reference appears. And that is
noteworthy just because of the profound sacer-
dotalism of the whole context of the Epistle.

On a careful review of the words before us
(verses 10–16), we are justified in the conclusion that the reference is, not to a Christian
institution at all but precisely to the Hebrew
ritual, in which Writer and readers still had part
as members of *the nation*. The thing in view is
an altar whose law was such that the sacerdotal
"ministers (οἱ λατρεύοντες) of the Tabernacle"
might not use its sacrifices for food. But why?

Not of course because they were not Christians, but because the sacrifices in question presented there were to be wholly "burned," "burned without the camp." The entire thought moves within the limits of the typical ceremonial. It deals with the holocaust which even the sacrificer might handle only to commit it to the fire; the victim whose destiny was to be—not eaten by the priestly family but carried outside the camp as wholly devoted for the people's sins.

It is possible, within the lines of the Levitical ritual, to interpret in more ways than one the " altar " in question. It may be the great altar, regarded in its special use on the Atonement Day (Lev. xvi.); not another structure than that used for other sacrifices, but that same altar regarded, for the moment, as if separated and alone, because of the awful speciality of the stern while merciful ritual of that great day. Or again, as it has been argued with learning and force,* the reference may be to the altar of incense, the golden altar of the Holiest, on which the blood not only of the atonement victims but of all sin-offerings was sprinkled; and every sacrifice so treated was regarded as a holocaust; no part of it was reserved for food. But in either case the altar in question is not of the

* By the Rev. James Burkitt, in *The Golden Altar: an Exposition of Hebrews xiii. 10, 11.*

Church but of the Tabernacle. The "we" of ver. 10 is the community in its Hebrew rather than in its Christian character.

So the whole thought centres itself in the supreme Sacrifice, as Antitype answering to type. Jesus is our holocaust, wholly sacrificed for our sins. His sacrifice involved in its awful ritual the shame and agony of rejection by His own, excommunication from "the camp" of the chosen. Then let the Hebrew believer, "receiving that inestimable benefit," be ready also to follow his Redeemer's steps in rejection and in shame. Let him also be prepared for casting out by priest and scribe. Let his yearning heart, with whatever anguish, inure itself to the thought that the beloved "city of his solemnities" is not the final and enduring Jerusalem. Let his "thoughts to heaven the steadier rise," as he looks, like Abraham before him, to "God's great town in the unknown land," where sits on high the Mediator of the New Covenant, the "Priest upon His throne."

13

Last Words

Hebrews 13: 15-25

THE connexion of ver. 15 with the antecedent context is suggestive. We have been led to a contemplation of the Lord Jesus in His character as Antitype and Fulfilment of the holocaust, of the Levitical atonement. Even as the chief animal victim of the old covenant, the symbolical bearer of the sins of Israel, was carried "outside the camp" to be consumed, so our Victim was led "outside the gate" of the city to His death, that there, by His blood-shedding, by His absolute and perfect self-immolation in our stead, He might "hallow His people," bringing them forgiven and welcomed back to God. The point of the dread ritual of Calvary here specially emphasized is just this, that He "suffered outside the gate." The old Israel, guiltily unknowing, fulfilled the type in the Antitype by refusing Him place even to die within the sacred city. He, in His love for the new Israel, that He might in every particular be and do what was foreshadowed for Him, refused not to submit to that supreme rejection.

From this the apostolic Writer draws two messages for his readers. First (ver. 13) they are to follow the Lord outside, willing to be rejected like Him and because of Him. They are to be patient, for His sake, when they are "put out of the synagogues" and reproached as traitors to Moses. They are by faith to conquer the cry of their human hearts as they crave perpetuity for the beloved past; they are to remember (ver. 14), as they issue from the old covenant's gate into what seems the wild, that "Jerusalem that now is" was built for time only, and that they belong to the city of eternity, where their High Priest sits on His throne to bless them now and welcome them hereafter. Then, secondly and therefore (ver. 15), they are to use Him now and for ever as their one sacerdotal Mediator. By Him, not by the Aaronic ministry, they are to bring their sacrifices to God. They are to accept exclusion and to turn it into inclusion, into a shutting-up of all their hopes and all their worship into their glorious Christ. And what now is their altar-ritual to be? It is to be twofold; the offering of praise, "the fruit of lips that confess" the glory of "His Name," and then the sacrifice

of self and its possessions for others for His sake
(ver. 16); "doing good, and communicating"
blessings; for these are "altar-sacrifices ($\theta v\sigma iai$)
with which God is well pleased."

Such, if we are right, is the connexion. The
Lord, rejected, that He might die for us after a
manner faithful to the prophetic type, is to be
the Hebrew disciple's example of patience when
he too is rejected. Such rejection is only to
unite him the more closely to the Christ as
his way to God, his Mediator for all the praise
and all the unselfish service which is to fill
his dedicated life.

The lesson was special for the believing
Hebrew then. But it has its meaning for all
time. In one way or another the true follower
of the crucified and rejected Redeemer must
stand ready for cross and for exclusion, so far
as he is called upon by his faith to break with
all ultimate and absolute allegiance save to
"Jesus Christ and Him crucified." He has to
recollect, on one account or another, that he
too belongs to the invisible order, to the "citi-
zenship that is in heaven," and not to any visible
polity as if it were final, as if it were his spirit's
goal. But then he too is to make this detach-
ment and separation only a fresh means to unite
him to his great High Priest for a self-sacrificial
life in Him. He is to be no frowning sectary,

saying, "I am holier than thou." He is to be simply a Christian, to whom, whatever the world may say, or the world-element in the Church, Christ the crucified is Lord indeed.

Following these appeals, in a connexion which we can trace, the thought passes (ver. 17) to the Christian Ministry. "Outside the gate" of the old order, the disciple finds himself at once not an isolated unit but included in *a new order*. He is one of a spiritual community, which has of course its system, for it has to cohere and to operate. It has amidst it its "leaders," its ἡγούμενοι, its pastoral guides and watchmen, a recognized institution, which always as such (though always the more as it is more true to its ideal) claims the obedience, the loyalty, the subordination, of the multitude who are not "leaders." These "leaders" are set before us as bearing a Divine commission, for we read that they "must *give account*." So qualified, not as assertors of themselves but as servants and agents of God, they watch for souls, with a vigilance loving and tender, asking for response.

Such an ideal of the Christian Ministry is as remote as possible from that of a sacerdotal caste, or indeed of anything that has to do with a harsh and perfunctory officialism. Its position is totally different from that of an agency of mediation between man and God, between the Church and

her Lord. We have one passing note of this in
the fact, present in other Epistles as in this, that
the Ministry is addressed and greeted through
the Church rather than the Church through the
Ministry. See below, ver. 24 : "Salute your
leaders." If we may put it so, the Christian
clergy are so far from being the sole deliverers of
the apostolic writings to the people that the people
rather have to deliver such messages to the clergy.

Yet on the other hand this passage is one of
the many which set the Christian Ministry before
us as a vital factor in the life of the Church, an
institution which has its life from above, not
from the will of the community but from the
gift of God. In their anxiety to avoid distor-
tions and exaggerations of the ministerial idea
many Christians have failed to give adequate
place in thought to its essentially Divine origin
and commission. A passage like this should
correct such a reaction. There is in the Church,
by the will of God, a "leadership," recognizable,
authentic, not arbitrary yet authoritative, not
mediatorial yet pastoral. It is never designed
indeed to come really between the believing soul
and the ever-present Lord. Yet it is appointed
as the normal human agency by which He works
for the soul, not only in the solemn ministration of His great ordinances of blessing but in
spiritual assistance and guidance as well. It

will be the pastor's folly if he so insists upon
the imagery of shepherding as to forget for one
moment that the "sheep" are also, and in a
larger aspect, his equal brethren and sisters,
" the sons and daughters of the Lord Almighty."
It will be his folly, and the ruin of his true
authority, if he forgets in any part of his service
that he is not the master but the servant of the
Church. If in his "guidance" he dares to
domineer, and if in his teaching he takes the
tone of one who can *dictate* any point of faith
or duty, on his own authority, apart from the
Word of God, he is fatally mistaking his whole
function. Nevertheless he is called to be a
" leader," with the responsibilities and duties
of a leader. This thought is to keep him always
humble, and always intently on the watch
over his own life. But it is to be present
also to the members of the Church, to remind
them always to *tend towards* that generous
" obedience " with which Christian freedom safe-
guards Christian order. The Church is never to
forget the responsibility of the Ministry ; it is to
assist the Ministry in its true discharge. For in
this also " we are members one of another."

The closing sentences of the great Letter
(ver. 18 and onwards) call for little detailed
explanation, with one great exception. The

Writer asks for intercessory prayer for himself
and his colleagues, in the accent of one who
knows his own unreserved desire (ver. 18) to
keep his whole "life-walk honourable," καλῶς
ἀναστρέφεσθαι. He asks specially for this help,
with a view to his own speedier return to his
disciples (ver. 19), an allusion which we cannot
now explain for certain. At the very end
(verses 22–25), with a noble modesty, in the
tone of the true Christian leader, drawing, not
driving, he asks for "patience" over his "appeal"
(παράκλησις), his solemn call for loyalty to the
Christ of God under all the trials of the time.

He has "used brevity" (διὰ βραχέων) in
writing; he might have expanded the vast theme
indefinitely; he has only given them its essentials. Then he makes his one personal reference, abruptly, as if speaking about well-known
circumstances; Timotheus (ver. 23) has been
released from prison, and is on his way to join
the Writer, and the two may hope to visit the
Hebrews together again. Then follows the
greeting to the pastors through the Church; and
then a message of love sent by "those from Italy,"
that is to say, as the familiar idiom suggests,
brethren resident in Italy who send their
greeting from it; an allusion over which endless
conjectures may gather but which must always
remain uncertain. The last word is the blessing

of grace. "Grace"—the holy effect upon the
Church, and upon the saint, of "God for us"
and "God in us"—"be with you all."

We have thus followed this final passage to
its end, but making, as the reader will have
seen, [one great omission. The twentieth and
twenty-first verses stand by themselves, with
such an elevation of their own, with such a
tranquil majesty of diction, with such a pregnant
depth of import, that I could not but reserve
my brief comment on them to the very last in
these attempts to carry "Messages from the
Epistle to the Hebrews."

"Now the God of peace, who hath brought
again from the dead the Shepherd of the sheep,
that great Shepherd, with blood of covenant
eternal, even our Lord Jesus—may He perfect
you in all good unto the doing of His will, doing
in you that which is acceptable before Him, by
means of Jesus Christ; to whom be the glory
to the ages of the ages. Amen."

Here is one of the greatest, if not the greatest,
of the benedictory prayers of the Bible. At
every turn it sets before us truths of the first
order, woven into one wonderful texture. It
presents to us our God as "the God of peace,"
the God who has welcomed us to reconciliation
and is now and for ever reconciled; at peace

with us and we with Him. It sets full in view
the supreme fact upon which that certainty
reposes, the Resurrection of His Christ, recorded
here and only here in the long Epistle, as the
act and deed by which the Father sealed before
the universe His acceptance of the Son for us.
It connects that Resurrection with its mighty
antecedent, the atoning Death, in words pregnant with the truths characteristic of the Epistle ;
the Lord, the great Shepherd, was "brought
again from the dead" (the phrase is reminiscent
of Isa. lxiii. 11, with its memories of Moses
and the ascent of Israel from the parted waters),
"in the blood" (as it were attended, authen-
ticated, entitled, by the blood) "of covenant
eternal," that supreme Compact of Divine love of
which twice over (chapters viii., x.) the Epistle
has spoken ; under which, for the slain Mediator's
sake, God both forgives iniquity and transfigures
the will of the forgiven. Then the prayer
follows upon these mighty premisses. The
Teacher asks, with the authority of an inspired
benediction, that this God of peace, of covenant,
of the crucified and risen Lord Jesus, would
carry out the covenant-promise in His new Israel
to the full. May He "perfect" them, that is
to say, equip them on every side with every
requisite of grace, for the supreme purpose of
their existence, the doing of His will in everything.

May He so inhabit and inform them, through
His Son, by His Spirit, that He shall be the
will within their will, the force beneath their
weakness, "working in them to will and to do
for His good pleasure's sake" (Phil. ii. 13). To
Him, the Father, be glory for ever. To Him,
the Son, be glory for ever. Who shall decide,
and who need decide, to which Divine Person
the relative pronoun ᾧ precisely attaches?
The glory is to the Father in the Son, to the
Son in the Father.

One closing word remains. Observe this
designation just here applied to the Lord Jesus
Christ; "the Shepherd, the great Shepherd, of
the sheep." It is noteworthy, because in our
Epistle it stands here quite alone. We have
had the Christ of God presented to us throughout under the totally different character of the
High Priest, the great Self-Immolator of the
Cross, now exalted in the glory of His High
Priesthood to be the Giver of blessing from the
Throne. To Him in that sublime aspect the
thought of the Hebrew believer, so sorely tempted
to look away from Him, to look backward to
the old and ended order, has been steadily
directed, for spiritual rest of conscience and for
loyalty of will. But here, true to that *habit*
of the Bible, if the word may be used, with
which it accumulates on Him the most diverse

titles in the effort to set forth His fulness, the Writer exchanges all this range of thought for the one endearing designation of the SHEPHERD of the sheep. It was as such that He went down to death, giving for the flock His life. It was as such that He is "brought again," to rescue, to watch, to feed, to guide His beloved charge, " in the power of life indissoluble."

Not without purpose surely was the Lord left pictured thus in the view of His tried and tempted followers. In the region of conviction and contemplation He was to shine always before them as the High Priest upon His throne, the more than fulfilment of every type and shadow, the goal of Prophecy, " the end of the Law." But He was to be all this as being also, close beside them, their Shepherd, great and good. He was to be with them in the pasture, and in the desert, and in the valley of the shadow of death. They had followed Him indeed as their Sacrifice without the gate. But precisely there He took to Himself His resurrection-life, to be their Companion and their Watcher for evermore. The Lord was their Shepherd, and He is ours; they should not, and we shall not, want.